HEALING THE ADDICTIVE MIND

HEALING THE ADDICTIVE MIND

LEE L. JAMPOLSKY, PH.D.

CELESTIAL ARTS
BERKELEY, CALIFORNIA

CELESTIAL ARTS
P.O. Box 7327
Berkeley, California 94707

Cover design by Ken Scott
Text design by Jeff Brandenburg
Composition by ImageComp

Library of Congress Cataloging-in-Publication Data

Jampolsky, Lee L., b. 1957
        Healing the addictive mind / Lee L. Jampolsky.
            p.   cm.
        Includes bibliographical references.
        ISBN 0–89087–623–1
        1. Compulsive behavior. 2. Self-respect. I. Title.
    RC533.J36 1991   90–2171
    616.86—dc20   CIP

First Printing, 1991

0 9 8 7 6 5
95 94

Manufactured in the United States of America

Contents

Preface ix

Foreword xi

Introduction xiii

CHAPTER ONE

The Fallacy of Looking Outside of Ourselves
   for Happiness 1
   What Addiction Is 1
   The Invitation to Love 3
   The Disease Controversy..4
   I'm Afraid of You Because You're Just Like Me 5
   Who We Are Versus Who Our Egos Tell Us We Are 8
   On Happiness 11
   The Fallacy of "Not Being Enough" 14
   Denial: The Foundation of Addiction 16
   The Ego's Plan: Deny It and It Will Disappear 16
   Projection..17
   The Two Faces of Projection 19

CHAPTER TWO

The Structure of the Addictive Thought System 23
   The Addictive Thought System 24
   On Fear 24
   On Living in the Past or the Future 29
   On Judgment 32
   On Scarcity 35

CHAPTER THREE

The Core Beliefs of the Addictive Thought System 39
   The Two Forms of Communication 50

CHAPTER FOUR

The Structure of the Love-Based Thought System 53

The Love-Based Thought System 54
On Love 55
On the Present Moment 58
On Acceptance 63
On Abundance 66

CHAPTER FIVE

The Core Beliefs of the Love-Based Thought System 71

Comparison of the Addictive Thought System and the
    Love-Based Thought System 83
Beliefs of the Addictive Thought System 84
Beliefs of the Love-Based Thought System 85

CHAPTER SIX

Addiction and the Fear of Intimacy 87

Family Roles and the Fear of Love 88
Locking Love Out 90
On Responsibility 91
The Fallacy of "I'm Not Okay the Way I Am" 92
Addiction and the Carrot Syndrome 93
Attack, Defense, and Addiction 94
The Alternative to Attack and Defense 95
The Underpinnings of Attack and Defense 96
Trust Versus trust 99

CHAPTER SEVEN

Learning To Love Ourselves 103

Irrational Beliefs of the Addicted Mind 103
Irrational Beliefs of the Ego 112
Sane Beliefs of Love-Based Thinking 113
Codependency as Addiction 113
Core Beliefs of Codependency 115
Letting Go: Giving Forgiveness a Place To Happen 117
Affirming Who You Are 119
Truths About Myself 120

CHAPTER EIGHT

Growing as a Couple: Moving from Fear to Love 121

Thoughts That Encourage Couples To Stay Stuck 126
Thoughts That Encourage Couples To Open to Love 127

DAILY LESSONS 129

Introduction to Daily Lessons 131
How To Proceed with the Daily Lessons 131
Daily Lessons (1–21). 133

Epilogue 161

About the Author 163

Preface

Many of the central ideas in this book come from *A Course In Miracles* (*ACIM*), a three-volume, self-taught course published by the Foundation for Inner Peace. The daily lessons, in boldface type in Part Two, are quotes from *ACIM*, printed here with permission of the holder of the copyright, its publisher.

Though many teachings and writings have influenced my life, *ACIM* has been the most influential; it teaches me to examine how I think about and perceive myself and the world. *ACIM* never asks that the reader believe what it posits, but rather asks that the reader practice the principles on a daily basis. I invite you to approach this book in the same spirit. I do not ask that you immediately believe all that is discussed, for much of it may seem foreign. I simply ask that you practice the principles and pay attention to what results.

It is my sincere hope that by reading and practicing the principles set forth in this book you will be able to identify and gently remove the obstacles that block an awareness of love.

> Your task is not to seek for love,
> but merely to seek and find
> all of the barriers within yourself
> that you have built against it.
>
> —*A Course in Miracles*

Foreword

Ten years ago the thought of writing a book about addiction would have truly been the pot calling the kettle black. If you added the possibility that I would share any of my own personal history in an open and honest way, I would have been overcome by feelings of shame so deep that I no doubt would have tried to hide in one of my many addictions. Perhaps I would have chosen the more acceptable addiction that I had mastered: "Overachieve and nobody will see my incompetence and shame." Or perhaps I would have turned to drugs to numb my pain, something I did for so many years that self-medicating my pain had become as "normal" as relieving an itch by scratching it. Perhaps I would have turned to finding another romantic relationship to disappear into, thinking that another person could somehow rescue me from my struggle.

Even five years ago I would have been filled with thoughts such as: "I'm such a hypocrite. Here I am preaching all of this 'self-help' material and I am far from being able to help myself."

Much of my life I have been fighting feelings of low self-esteem. It has been easier for me to condemn myself than it has been to love myself. My mood becomes weighted with depression of days past when I think of the thousands of times I have chained myself to pain with self-critical thoughts. So many times did I long for the emptiness within me to be filled, yet at the same moment I believed that this void could never be filled. For years I settled for the momentary relief that my many addictions seemed to offer me.

Today I write this foreword, having completed the rest of the book. In the book I share my thoughts, my feelings, and my struggle in loosening the hold of addiction on my life. I share with you examples from my life and from the lives of many people with whom I have been fortunate enough to work. I have not completed my journey; I am still a traveler. I still stumble and fall, yet I also continue to unfold knowing myself. If each year that passes I can love who I am a little more, and become willing to trust where I once ran to an addiction, I know that I have made progress.

I offer you not a panacea to addiction but rather a means to better know and accept yourself. It is my belief that where there is acceptance and love, there is no need for addiction.

As I read through the pages of this book I am deeply grateful. I am thankful to all those who have so courageously and intimately shared their lives with me, both professionally and personally. The information in the vignettes of clients that I have included have been altered in order to ensure confidentiality. All names, identifying information, and other factors have been changed. Many of the stories are composite sketches. Any resemblance that you may find between the vignette and somebody that you know is purely coincidental.

Introduction

Most of us find ourselves walking through our lives experiencing only fragmented moments of peace of mind. We spend our lives thinking that the next accomplishment, relationship, drug, or dollar will bring us the happiness and contentment for which we long. We end up like hungry tigers chasing their tails, running in circles and becoming more frustrated and ferocious with each step.

The goal of this book is to assist you in experiencing what you really want: peace of mind.

As a psychologist working with addiction, and in my own life, I have found that addictive behavior is not limited to a reliance on alcohol or other drugs. It is my belief that addiction to chemical substances is a metaphor for our current human condition. The roots of addiction lie not in a bottle, a vial, or a syringe. The roots of addiction can be seen in our search for happiness in something outside of ourselves, be it drugs, relationships, or new shiny cars. As long as we are looking for happiness in the world, rather than in our own minds, we may be in the throes of addiction. While our minds are in the vicious cycle of addiction, peace of mind remains out of reach.

It is my belief that inner peace is a matter of choice, if only we know what the choices are and how to choose. Most of my life I walked through the world convincing myself that I had endless decisions to make, each of which was all-important. Most of the time, no matter what choice I made, I was still in conflict. Slowly I am learning to distinguish between what causes me to stay fearful and what releases me to experience more joy in my life. In this book I share with you what I believe the choices are and how to choose.

My hope is that by the time you are finished with this book, you will have the tools to more consistently choose peace of mind.

In this book addiction is perhaps defined in a broader sense than you are accustomed to. Addiction is addressed as a human condition that affects most people. If, like me, you have ever felt that your happiness was dependent on someone else's behavior, getting some new possession or more money, being in a certain place, having sex, or a specific outcome to a situation, this book is addressed to you.

Much of what I present may at first seem confusing or debatable. This reaction may indicate that you are trying to fit something new into an old schema, or have become stuck in your view of the world. Because much of the material presented in this book may be new to your way of thinking, certain topics are repeated in various forms. This repetition ensures that you give your mind a chance to question old negative patterns of thought.

To get the most out of this book, try to approach the material with fresh eyes and an open mind. At times I will invite you to examine your thoughts and to question some of the beliefs and assumptions that you have about yourself and the world. Through self-exploration you will have the opportunity to change your experience by examining and changing your beliefs and assumptions. The goal of this book is simple: it is to assist you in recognizing and listening to the presence of love, which is in us all.

I decided to write this book after struggling with my own addictions and after years of working with individuals and families struggling with theirs. I grew up in an alcoholic family and continue to work through many of the issues that this created. In my work I have found that most families are affected by addiction in some form. The patterns of behavior of family members affected by addiction are, individually and collectively, both predictable and tragic. I also have witnessed that recovery from addiction can be a doorway to awakening to love. Unfortunately, I also have seen many people, including myself, simply trade one addiction for another and call it recovery, burying love deeper in darkness. After I no longer used alcohol and other drugs, I fell prey to workaholism. I have come to believe that what determines the difference between awakening to love and trading addictions is the extent to which we examine our fundamental beliefs about ourselves and the world.

There have been many uses of the word *addiction*, most in relation to chemical dependency. One of my goals with this book is to have you become more aware of the breadth of addiction. When you see the word *addiction* in this book, you may mentally replace it with the phrase, "pursuing happiness in things (people, places, substances) external to myself." The professional community is in the process of shifting the definition of addiction so that it is broader. For example, leading medical experts in chemical dependency define addiction as "continued compulsive use despite adverse consequences." I feel that such a definition can be applied equally well to addiction to money, possessions, food, work, relationships, sex—or any other thing.

I believe that most of us, to some degree, have pockets of addiction in our lives. The extent to which we are stuck in our addictive patterns is the extent to which we inhibit our potential to love. If you have become tired of attempting to find hiding places from the world, long for relief from running faster on the treadmill, or realize that more does not equal happier, then this book is addressed to you.

This book is divided into two parts. The first section offers you an understanding of what addiction is and how it affects our lives. In the second section, specific daily lessons are presented that are designed to help you choose peace more consistently in your life.

LEE L. JAMPOLSKY, PH.D.
Carmel, California
April 1990

To Carny and Jalena.

There have been no greater
gifts in my life than the two of you.

CHAPTER ONE

The Fallacy of Looking Outside of Ourselves for Happiness

*A*ddiction is a familiar word, yet what exactly does the word mean? It is safe to say that no addict woke up one morning and set out to become as addicted as he or she possibly could. Addiction is more covert and sly, and seems to sneak into a person's life through the back door. Most people would not call themselves addicts, yet it is my observation that addictive behavior is prevalent in our society.

When we find ourselves frustrated, angry, and unhappy, we probably don't recognize that what is occurring could be the process of addiction. And if we don't recognize an addiction, we dig a deeper hole for ourself in an attempt to escape the uncomfortable feelings. It is time to stop running away from addiction and to begin to look closer at just what addiction is.

WHAT ADDICTION IS

I had been seeing Peter in my practice for about three months when, during a session, he began crying uncontrollably. I was moved by the depth of his crying. The sounds that left his mouth sounded ancient, as though they had lain chained in dark isolation for centuries. Peter struggled to speak through his tears, as if the familiarity of words would bring him out of the pain that so enveloped him. But words would not come, and only the despair of

1

deep loneliness filled the room. Then for a moment Peter emerged from the hold of his pain, as if gasping for air in a sea of unknown depth, and whispered from his tears the only words he could say: "I'm so afraid."

Peter had been addicted to cocaine for seven years. Prior to my seeing him he had not used any mind-altering substance for one year. He had gone to a well-known 28-day recovery program. Peter was 32 years old, married, a lawyer, had plenty of money, lived in a beautiful home, and yet felt that there was "something missing." At the time Peter began to see me, he stated, "I have everything going for me and I don't use drugs anymore—and I'm still not happy."

Peter came to find that the "something missing" he described was the awareness and experience of love. What kept him from love was his constant pursuit of happiness in things external to himself, which, in turn, covered up his deep feelings of emptiness and aloneness. It was not until the session just described that Peter even knew that he felt alone and separate from everybody and everything. Cocaine had been a dam, holding back the waters of loneliness. His stopping the use of cocaine had been the first step, and now Peter was face to face with his worst fear: his aloneness.

Peter, believed, deep down, as many of us do, that he was alone and isolated in a cruel and punishing world. From this largely repressed belief Peter set out to fill this void of emptiness. He began looking outside of himself for things that he mistakenly thought would make him feel whole. In so doing he began his downward spiral in addiction. It was in the session just described that Peter began to realize that neither drugs nor money nor relationships could fill the void, the emptiness that he felt. Only removing the blocks to love in his own mind could begin to heal him and return him to wholeness.

In the months following this session, Peter began to see that his addiction had nothing to do with weakness or willpower. He began to see that his addiction to cocaine was simply a part of his addictive search for satisfaction and gratification in things external to himself.

Many people in our society look at people addicted to alcohol or other drugs as weak and morally inferior. It was the great anthropologist Gregory Bateson that first suggested differently. He painted a picture of the addict as a person who had a spiritual thirst, a sense of knowing that there was something more. The addict found that alcohol or other drugs momentarily and partially slaked this thirst and became confused. Peter, though in deep pain, began to reconnect with his feeling that there must be something more. Through recognizing this spiritual longing, he began to look inside himself. Inspired by Peter's journey, I wrote the following:

THE QUIET PLACE INSIDE

The tangled roots of addiction
begin in my mind
when I believe that the world is
a land of trinkets promising happiness.

In this world I feel trapped,
surrounded by a moat of deep and shadowy
waters of loneliness and despair.
The knurled, spiny roots of addiction encase and
squeeze my heart, forcing the
memory of love to fade into darkness.

Let me today come to realize
that there is a quiet place inside of me,
a place kept safe for me,
where love lies protected and unharmed.

Today my awareness of love shines light
through the darkness of addiction.
The light of love is who I am.
Today I will take time to be still
and listen to the truth about who I am.

THE INVITATION TO LOVE

Peter began to see how his aloneness and his addiction fed one another. To avoid his sense of aloneness he would look beyond himself for happiness, thus entering an addictive pattern. The more he did this, the more alone he felt, which caused him to escalate his dead-end search. That one day, sitting across from me in my office, he confronted the emptiness that he had tried so hard to cover up.

In so doing he took the first step toward being able to allow love in his life.

Many of us in our adult lives have shied away from spirituality. For some, negative experiences with religion as children caused us to turn away from God. I define the recovery from addiction as the process of awakening to love. This is the same way that I would define any spiritual journey. Opening the heart to love is the highest human experience, and is what undoing addiction is about.

When we look to anything other than our own minds for happiness, we deny love. We can't hide in our addiction and experience love at the same time. This is indeed an interesting phenomenon, because our addiction tells us quite the opposite. Our addiction plays the "If . . . then . . . " game. "If I get so-and-so to behave, then I will feel loved." "If I get high, then I will not be so angry and I will be able to love my spouse." These endless "if . . . thens" cause us to never feel the love that is ever-present in the quiet of our hearts. As we begin to quiet the chatter of the "If . . . then game," the awareness of love returns. Ask yourself, How would my awareness of myself and the world change this instant if I simply put all of my energy into welcoming love into my life?

Peter and I ended his session that day with him visualizing a small white light in the center of his heart. Slowly, he allowed that white light to fill his heart until it could not contain the light any longer. He allowed the white light to spread throughout his body until the boundary of his skin was not a sufficient boundary and this warm, peaceful white light began to surround him in a cocoon of light. I saw his tear-stained face give birth to a gentle, barely visible smile. I knew at that moment that he recognized love, and that the seeds of his healing had been planted. His feelings of aloneness had not vanished, but his perception of it had changed that day. Peter had found that the depth of his aloneness was shallow in comparison with the boundless depth of love. As I watched him surround himself with love, I was reminded of something that Hugh Prather once wrote: "Learning to love yourself is the definition of change."

THE DISEASE CONTROVERSY

Because many people reading this book may have an opinion as to whether chemical dependency (and codependency) is a disease, it is important to briefly address this area. In the past few years there has been increasing controversy as to what constitutes a disease. I am not interested, in this book, in adding fuel to the already raging fire of the debate. Rather, it is my purpose to provide a broader perspective as to the origin, progression, and recovery from all addictive behaviors.

I look at the word *disease* and see a word that describes the present state of "dis-ease" of the majority of human beings. In this book I suggest that the root of this dis-ease is our addictive thought system. Many people have approached addiction from the outside in: describing the behavior and then trying to stop it. I suggest a reversal to this approach and view addiction from the inside out: identifying and then changing the thoughts and beliefs that led us into the addictive experience.

With chemical dependency I feel that the disease concept serves an extremely useful role, regardless of future confirmation or rejection of the scientific validity of the disease model. Simply put, in early recovery the disease concept allows the individual and family to let go of some blame, condemnation, judgment, and guilt. If saying a person has a disease allows that person to look within, in the present moment, and say, "I have a choice now as to how to live my life," then I am all for it. Conversely, if saying a person has a disease means that person shucks responsibility for his or her life, then I am against it. In short, if a person says, "I have a disease" the next statement ideally will be "and I have a choice as to how to live my life."

I'M AFRAID OF YOU BECAUSE YOU'RE JUST LIKE ME

In my research, as well as in my general outlook on life, I have tried to take a road different from the one to which we are usually directed. Most of us are given assignments in school with such instructions as "Compare and contrast," or "Give a critical analysis." Though these skills have value, use of them reveals only a partial, a limited, picture. When we try to compartmentalize someone or something, we miss the true nature of what we are viewing.

When I approached my doctoral dissertation, I thought that there had to be a method better than comparing, contrasting, or analyzing the topic I explored. I found that traditional research made some of the same mistakes we all make: when we approach something new, we often try to make a square peg fit into a round hole. To make it fit, we must cut off the corners. I mentally gave myself instructions preceded by phrases such as *Find the commonalties between*, or *Seek the similarities and areas of integration*. I saw that this approach to research yielded much richer information for me, though it was often more difficult to undertake. After years of Western education, it was much easier for me to dissect, find differences, and discard, than it was to search for similarities. As I applied my new instructions to myself in research, I also found myself applying this approach to situations that arose in my personal life. I was pleasantly surprised to notice that I experienced a greater sense of inner calm. I found that when I compartmentalized, analyzed, and separated people, I felt more fear and isolation. When I saw commonalities and similarities between myself and others, even though they were sometimes painful, I felt more love and connectedness.

It is my belief that we are all teachers and students of one another, and that we are never finished in either role. Some time ago a great teacher came to see me disguised as a patient. I was an intern in a low-fee community counseling center when Tom came to see me as a patient. The consulting rooms were quite small, and as Tom entered the room, the smell of urine filled the air. Tom looked and smelled like he had not bathed for three months. In our first session Tom did little else but alternate between blank stares and hysterical laughter. He was missing most of his teeth, and his mouth was dry and cracked. His dirty, matted hair hung down over his unshaven face. This was early in my career, and I had had little experience with patients who didn't in some way resemble me and my upper middle class upbringing. Tom had grown up with a mother who had punished him regardless of what he did. He had never received a clear or esteeming message about anything. The accumulation of mixed and negative messages had paralyzed Tom. In addition, Tom's father had left when Tom was five. His mother had told him that his father's leaving was his fault. Tom's mother had been a maid and frequently would get fired, causing them to have to move from one transient hotel to another. She frequently had told Tom, "If I didn't have you, I wouldn't have any of these problems."

Tom was different from me and I was afraid of him. It wasn't that I thought that he would hurt me; I was just afraid of his difference. That first session I saw no similarities between Tom and myself. I met that week with my supervisor and other colleagues to get their opinions. They were helpful, but I somehow still felt fear and dreaded being in the same room with Tom. I was to see Tom three times a week for the next month. Things did not seem to get any better, and I thought that perhaps I should refer Tom to someone else. Yet I knew that Tom already had been bounced around the mental health system. He had been diagnosed as having a borderline personality disorder, and thus was seen as an unco-operative patient. It seemed as though I was having problems. I associated Tom with the stench of old urine, hardly a good foundation for a therapeutic relationship.

Somewhere in the second month of my seeing Tom, a miracle occurred. I define a miracle as a shift in perception that allows a person to experience peace and joining where conflict and separation once were.

Instead of going over case notes and trying to figure out what was "wrong" with Tom and how I was supposed to "fix" him, I sat in quiet with my eyes closed and asked for guidance in my work with Tom. As I walked into the waiting room to greet Tom, I began to feel loneliness inside me. As Tom sat down our eyes connected, and I saw my own isolation and despair in his eyes. This was the thing of which I really had been afraid. I had focused upon how different he was from me, but what I had been afraid of was how he was just like me. For most of my life I had repressed my deep sense of loneliness. Though to an outside observer I would probably have appeared "successful," I almost always felt a sense of being on the outside looking in.

In a moment our differences melted away. We sat in the nakedness of who we were. During the session he still laughed in his odd way, he still smelled like urine, but the feeling in the room had changed. The focus had shifted from my being aware of our differences to my being aware of our commonality. In the following sessions fear left and compassion entered. Critical analysis left and mutual trust grew.

Tom and I spent a few hours together each week for about a year. During that time he was able to tell me about his painful family history and the isolation of his existence. His blank stares and hysterical laughter gave way to tears of both pain and joy. Little changed in his appearance, yet there was inner change. I will never forget our last meeting. We stood in the middle of the room, embracing for several minutes. During this time I was aware of nothing but my compassion for Tom and our journey together toward awakening to love. He stepped back, grinning with his toothless smile, and said, "Now you smell like me." We both laughed, because we knew that neither of us had been aware of the same smell that originally had made me want to run away from him. Somehow smelling alike was a fitting way for us to part.

My experience with Tom brought home a few key points that I now try to remember in my daily life:

Guidelines To Follow in Getting To Know Myself

1. When I am focusing on differences, it is often because I'm afraid of something in myself.
2. Dwelling on differences creates distance and increases fear.
3. Concentrating on commonalities develops compassion and understanding, while increasing love.
4. When I am judging another person, it is a good indication that it's time to look at what I am denying about myself.
5. When I become attached to fixing or changing another person, I am entering into the world of addiction by seeing my happiness as dependent upon another person's behavior.

WHO WE ARE VERSUS WHO OUR EGOS TELL US WE ARE

The preceding discussion on the varying experiences yielded by focusing on differences or on commonalities begins to lay the groundwork for a discussion of the thought system of the ego. Let's look again at the definition of addiction we're using. Addiction is a compulsive and continuous searching for happiness outside of ourselves, despite the fact that contentment always eludes us.

More precisely, addiction is a continued compulsive external search, despite the fact that such a pursuit always leads us into pain and conflict. This is the way of the ego. If we are to reverse addictive behavior, we must begin to challenge the fundamental concepts of the ego, which are

1. *Guilt.* Guilt is the belief that we have done something wrong, bad, and unforgivable. Guilt is based upon the belief that the past is inescapable and determines the future.
2. *Shame.* As guilt increases, we not only believe that we have *done* something bad, we begin to believe that we *are* bad.
3. *Fear.* Because of guilt and shame and the resulting feelings that we have *done* something wrong and *are* something wrong, we then become plagued with a fear of punishment. For some this translates into the fear of God; for others this manifests itself in the belief that they don't deserve love.

Guilt, shame and fear do a war dance together that leaves us with anxiety and feelings of emptiness, incompleteness, and hopelessness. The ego keeps us from examining itself too closely by making us believe that guilt and shame are so strong and pervasive that we could not possibly get beyond them. Because of fear we run from looking within ourselves, and we begin to look to people, places, activities, and possessions for our happiness. It is in this external search for peace of mind that the ego pushes us towards our first steps in addiction.

When I was fifteen my father took my brother and me out to lunch at a nice restaurant near our home. He seemed preoccupied and a bit nervous. I was soon to find out why. This was the day he had chosen to tell us that my mother and he had decided to get a divorce.

Given the state of their marriage and the frequency of their arguments, an objective observer might have thought that this announcement would be no surprise. Yet it was a shock. As I heard the words come from my father's mouth my stomach felt as though the world were ending. Immediately I felt responsible, guilty, ashamed, and afraid. At the time I was probably most aware of being afraid. I don't remember showing any of these feelings to my brother, my father, or any other person. I kept them well hidden.

How I felt in the presence of my mother changed. I had always felt close to my mother, though sometimes enmeshed. Now I felt as though I had let her down, that somehow I could have done something to prevent all of this. My guilt seemed to match the depth of her pain.

Given a choice, I probably would have chosen to live with my mother. But I felt as though I had no choice, that I had to live with my mother because my father had abandoned me. In healing our relationship, my father and I have talked of this period in our lives many times in recent years. He is quite sure that he said that if I wanted to live with him that I could. Though I am sure that he did in fact say those words, the message that I heard from him was, "I am done with the family. I have my life to live. You stay at home and take care of your mother. Don't bother me." My brother, who was seventeen at the time, decided to move to Lake Tahoe. I didn't share my feelings with my mother because I felt that she was already in such grief that my problems would be too much for her. Because I made this assumption, I never let my mother know of my internal pain. In retrospect, it would have been healing for both of us if I had been able to let her know how the situation was affecting me.

The result was that I felt empty and alone. At the time I was going to a private high school. My grades dropped because I was often absent. Though I had previously experimented with drugs, my use increased. I was looking for some way to relieve the pain that I was feeling. Shortly after my parents' separation I was called into the headmaster's office, where he and the dean told me that though the school had never permanently expelled a student before, that they had decided that there was really no hope for my living up to the standards of the school. With the dubious honor of being the first kid to get kicked out of my school, my guilt and shame only increased.

It wasn't that I just felt guilty and ashamed; I was also terrified of looking at any aspect of what I was experiencing. I was afraid that my understanding of the headmaster's and the dean's message was correct: that I was worthless and doomed to failure. My guilt, shame and fear caused feelings of loneliness, emptiness, failure, and deep hopelessness. Most of all, I didn't feel worthy of love. As a result, I began the addictive cycle of looking to drugs for relief.

The following are quotes from *Accept This Gift: Selections from A Course In Miracles*, by Walsh and Vaughn.

Love and guilt cannot coexist,
and to accept one is to deny the other.

The end of guilt will never come
as long as you believe there is a reason for it.

For you must learn that guilt is always totally insane,
and has no reason.

Only your mind can produce fear.

You must have noticed an outstanding characteristic
of every end that the ego has accepted as its own.
When you have achieved it,
it has not satisfied you.
That is why the ego is forced to shift ceaselessly
from one goal to another,
so that you will continue to hope
it can yet offer you something.

The preceding quotes, especially the last, to me, are, what addiction is about. When we continue to shift from one goal (relationship, job, drug) to another, despite the fact that our goals never satisfy us, we are caught in the cycle of addiction.

ON HAPPINESS

The external search for happiness is pervasive in contemporary society. You can't watch more than fifteen minutes of commercial television without a series of advertisements telling you that you need some new and improved products in order to be happier. At a very early age you begin to form the core of the ego's addictive thought system: that you are fundamentally inadequate as you are, and need something outside of yourself to make you whole.

It is crucial to question the belief system of the ego. The addictive thought system is seriously flawed and never gives us lasting peace of mind. In contrast with the addictive thought system, the love-based thought system tells us that our natural state of mind is one of wholeness and peace.

In my work with newly recovering chemically dependent and codependent people, I am often amazed at the strength and irrationality of the addictive thought system. In giving a lecture one evening I was talking about happiness, and I began to notice people were either shaking their heads no or looked angry. I'm not quite over my need to have people like me, so I thought that I should inquire as to what was on people's minds. I asked a woman in the front row why she was shaking her head. She said that she thought I was nuts because I was talking as if people could be happy whenever they wanted, and that was simply not true. A man in the back agreed with her, stating that certain situations were beyond our control and that in such circumstances it would be "natural" to be upset and unhappy. I began to see the absurdity of the addictive thought system. We argue for our unhappiness (and our addictions) as if they were things that we want and need! We convince ourselves that the situation, not our thoughts, determine our experience.

Instead of continuing with the planned lecture, I went on to conduct an impromptu poll. I asked how many people thought that it was possible to be happy all of the time. Nobody raised his or her hand. I pursued my line of questioning and asked, "What about eighty percent of the time?" A few people raised their hands. "Do I hear sixty percent? How many people think that it is possible to be happy a mere sixty percent of the time?" A few more hands. As I continued, the largest group of people raised their hands at the fifty percent mark.

I'll let you in on a secret that the ego tries to keep hidden. When you are born into this world, there is no stamp, tattoo, contract, or other binding paper that states "This new being is limited to 52.31 percent happiness." The truth is

The only limitations on your happiness are the ones that you invent.

For many of us, this is hard to accept. It is much more convenient to place the responsibility for our happiness on something or someone else than it is to take personal responsibility for our happiness. I invite you to ask yourself a question and give it some thought: What do I need, that I don't have, in order to have peace of mind right now? Using the addictive thought system,—the ego's thought system—we would have an endless list: perhaps more money, a more attractive mate, a better job.

You may have noticed that I use the word *happiness* and the phrase *peace of mind* interchangeably. To me, the word *happiness* does not denote a constantly smiling face, for we certainly have more than one feeling and one expression. Yet it is possible to go through traumatic situations and still have peace of mind, and, in consequence, a sense of happiness. Tears and happiness are not mutually exclusive, if you are using the word to denote peace of mind. After all, if true happiness is not peace of mind, then what is?

At different times in my life I have had situations arise that I felt were most definitely limitations on my happiness. I have learned that these situations are limiting only to the extent that I perceive them to be. One of the most difficult of these situations was a physical disability.

When I was twenty-five I began to notice that I could not hear as well as before. After a series of tests the diagnosis was still unclear, and the prognosis was vague. All that the physicians could really tell me was that my hearing would most likely not get better, might stay the same, and probably would get progressively worse. I found myself becoming depressed because of the possibility of going deaf, even though I could still hear pretty well. At the time I was just finishing graduate school and entering an internship as a psychologist. I believed that my ears were to me what hands were to a pianist. I feared not being able to function in what I had trained so long to do. I saw even the prospect of losing my hearing as a limitation on my happiness.

Through looking very closely at my situation I decided to concentrate on letting go of the negative image of losing my hearing and put my energy into thoughts about my hearing loss that were healing. I was quite relieved, and even proud, that my hearing stabilized and I had no continuing loss. I went on in my profession and never felt that my hearing limited me in any significant way.

Seven years later I "fell out of remission" and had a sudden hearing loss; I could no longer hear my patients, talk on the phone, or function in my college teaching position. I felt that this was indeed a limitation on my happiness. I thought, If I can't hear, then I can't be happy. I have not given up on my hearing improving, but as of this writing I need to wear a hearing aid in each ear. Though the aids allow me to function fairly well, initially my ego had a hard time with the fact that I needed to wear them. I was attached to being "healthy and normal" and thought that nobody would want to see a deaf psychologist. I began to understand that the real healing that needed to take place was in my mind. My task was to find the lesson in what was occurring. I needed to come to believe that it was possible to be hearing impaired, a psychologist, and happy.

One thing that I have begun to learn is that there are far more ways to hear than simply through understanding words. I am now more aware of hearing with the "ear of the heart." I pay more attention to the "sounds" of love, pain, joy, and despair that lie beneath and beyond the content of words. I honor the internal voice of my intuition more than I used to. I am finding that what I once saw as a total limitation is quite possibly a gift. I am still hopeful of getting my physical hearing back, but I would not want to give up all of the other levels of hearing that I am learning. There are still times when I become depressed about my hearing and the possibility that the loss will continue to progress. But I am more able to catch myself and see that the only limitations my hearing loss place upon me are ones that I invent. I choose to identify with the lessons to be learned rather than the limitations to be invented.

THE FALLACY OF "NOT BEING ENOUGH"

Love-based thinking recognizes a simple fact:

> I lack nothing in order to be happy right now.

This is because there is no shortage of love. As soon as we buy into the addictive thought system and see ourselves as lacking and incomplete, we begin our addictive search. When we perceive ourselves as separate and alone in a world where there is only so much to go around, we become addicts trying to get "enough." Yet the addictive thought system deceives us. It holds out a carrot promising happiness, yet secretly has the motto There Is Never Enough.

I recently saw the movie *The Little Shop of Horrors*. The movie, perhaps unintentionally, provides a powerful and comical example of our addictive thought system. As the story opens a young man finds a small and unusual plant, which he begins to nurture. One day the young man accidentally cuts his finger and finds, to his amazement, that the small plant thrives on his blood. Wanting to keep the plant healthy, he continues to feed it blood, but the plant wants more and more. The bigger the plant grows, the more it wants. The plant is never satisfied and only becomes louder and more obnoxious with increased feeding. Eventually the plant is a monstrous piece of botany demanding, "FEED ME! FEED ME!" This is what the ego, with its addictive thought system, feverishly states.

When did the addictive thought system start? It began precisely at the moment when we began to view ourselves as something other than whole, loving beings. It is a premise of this book that the experience of love is not something to be achieved; it is to be remembered. Who we are,—love,—has never left; it simply has been covered up by the addictive thought system. We did not become incomplete at some point in our lives, we simply forgot who we were, and so began searching outside of ourselves for happiness.

> Peace of mind is not something to be "achieved."
>
> The memory of love is only a thought away.
>
> Love awaits only my welcome.

A short time ago, in my practice, I was seeing a thirty-five-year-old woman named Dianne. She, as did many of the people that I see, described herself as a recovering codependent. This day, as she repeatedly used the phrase "in my recovery," it began to sound like fingernails screeching against a blackboard. I was not sure why it bothered me so—I had often referred to myself as a recovering addict,—but I jotted down a few notes after our session, deciding to give it some thought later in the day. About thirty minutes into seeing my next patient (a "recovering addict"), though I was not even thinking about my previous patient, I heard myself say, "I don't see us as 'recovering addicts' as much as I see us as 'remembering human beings'." I began to see that the word recovery put my wholeness out in the future someplace. The word remembering reminded me that love had never abandoned me, it just had been covered up with layers of addictive thinking. Since that day I like to refer to myself as a "remembering human being," thus reminding myself that all I need to do is remember that I am whole and complete right now.

DENIAL: THE FOUNDATION OF ADDICTION

The word *denial* is used frequently in chemical dependency programs. Part of the problem of chemical dependency is denial that there is any problem. I do not know any chemically dependent person who hasn't engaged in denial. Unfortunately, denial keeps the addict in an irrational frame of mind, allowing him or her to continue in addiction.

The process of denial in addiction is not limited to the area of chemical dependency. With any addiction, in order for the ego to continue its obsessive quest for external gratification, our underlying wholeness must be denied. In other words, addiction cannot exist where love and wholeness are truly acknowledged. It is the denial of our underlying wholeness that is the foundation of addiction. If we experienced ourselves as whole, addiction would not occur, because we would feel complete, in and of ourselves. Unfortunately, we often remain blind to our own addictive patterns. We need to make a conscious effort to undo denial.

> Addiction is born out of thinking that we are
> less than whole.

> Today let me not see myself as limited in any way.
> Today may I stop denying love.

THE EGO'S PLAN: DENY IT AND IT WILL DISAPPEAR

The ego's backwards plan for our release from guilt has two key elements: denial and projection.

In the early 1980s I was living on a ranch in Marin county, about thirty miles north of San Francisco. The only service on the ranch was electricity. The water for the home came from a spring. The garbage that we accumulated needed to be either recycled, hauled to the dump, or put in the compost pile. I was in charge of the compost pile. I chose a spot for it near the house, close to where I liked to sit in the sun and read. About once a week I would take the garbage out and put it in the compost pile, diligently breaking up the larger pieces and mixing them into the earth. As time went on I became lazy and would just bury some of the larger pieces, not taking the time to break the material apart and mix it into the soil. One day, while reading in my favorite spot, I noticed the place was starting to smell like a dump. My laziness in just burying my garbage had ruined my ability to relax and enjoy my peaceful spot. A farmer I am not, but I did learn one simple rule: Burying something and forgetting it does not work.

One aspect of denial is thinking that if we bury our guilt, pushing it out of our awareness, we will be free of it. Not unlike my laziness with my compost pile, denial does not get rid of guilt. Denial produces fear.

PROJECTION

When you deny guilt and push it down, it starts eating away at you. The ego then looks for other ways to rid itself of guilt. In projection, the ego believes that if you unconsciously project your guilt away from yourself and onto someone else you will magically be freed. Instead, you increase your feelings of guilt, fear, and inadequacy.

This may be a difficult concept to grasp at first, not because it is complicated, but rather because we may have become so accustomed to tossing our guilt onto someone else. By so doing we think that we are safe from our most hidden fears. The problem is that this process of projection keeps us from looking at the source of the problem: our own mind.

Projection, and the behavior that is a result of it, is best illustrated with a metaphor. Imagine that we set up a movie projector in order to view a film. The lights dim and the film begins. About ten minutes into the movie you notice that I am fidgeting and appear uncomfortable. You ask me if I am okay, and I tell you that I don't like the movie. In fact, it is making me very uncomfortable. You know me as a rational person, so what I do next surprises you. I get up, walk over to the screen, and write on the screen, move it, even try to rip it. I don't like the movie, so I try to change the screen.

I suggest to you that each of us, sometimes on a daily basis, exhibits this insane behavior. Because we have a lot of company, nobody ever questions it. Let me begin to explain by asking you a question. If you don't like the movie, what are your more sane options? Though there are several answers, probably the most rational involve turning off the projector or changing the film. These answers reflect an understanding that the source of the image is not the screen. The image is projected onto the screen.

To understand how projection works in your daily life, imagine that the film projector is your mind and the film is your thoughts. By seeing life in this way we begin to recognize an important fact that we must embrace if we are to find peace of mind:

What you see is your own state of mind projected outwards.

Due to projection, you may believe that if you change other people to meet your specifications, then you will be happy. With this belief your actions are the same as my walking up to the movie screen and trying to change it. When we see negative things in other people it is often because we have denied that aspect of ourself; in an effort to rid ourself of it, we have projected it onto another person.

Even though on an intellectual level I understand projection, at times I still find myself acting insanely: trying to change others or seeing my dark side in them. For example, some years ago President Reagan was giving a speech and referred to Russia as an "evil empire." I remember that I became upset, because I felt that this statement was a projection. A few days later, as I was self-righteously telling a friend what I thought, I realized that I was making the same mistake that I was accusing the president of making: I was making Reagan *my* "evil empire." Sam Keen, in his book *Faces of the Enemy*, eloquently describes this process of creating images of the enemy out of our own repressed darkness. What he states about world conflict is also applicable to interpersonal conflict. According to Keen, "Healing begins when we cease playing the blame game, when we stop assigning responsibility for war to some mysterious external agency and dare to become conscious of our violent ways."

So when we blame another person for our unhappiness, it is a good indication that we must look at ourself and accept the responsibility that we have the ability to shape our own life. The more we are stuck in the habit of blaming others, the more we create a split between our conscious image of ourself as good, and our unconscious image of ourself as bad. The greater the split between our conscious and unconscious, the greater the need to project.

Projection can seem complex, but it is really quite simple. A few years back I acquired a new playful puppy. He would run from room to room, playing with whatever he found. One day I heard him fiercely barking and growling, something that I had never heard him do before. When I found him he was in the bathroom; the door had partially shut, revealing a full-length mirror. He was standing there, feet firmly planted, hair on his back raised, growling at his image in the mirror. I thought it was pretty silly of him not to realize he was threatening to attack his own image. But I guess that a lot of the time I am as silly as he is: I growl at another, not realizing that I am seeing repressed parts of myself.

THE TWO FACES OF PROJECTION

Projection has two primary forms of presenting itself: special hate and special love relationships.

In a special hate relationship we create a stage to play out the blame game. We take our own self-hatred, remorse, guilt, shame, and fear, and transfer it onto another. The goal of the game is to make another responsible for our misery. In the special hate relationship we also play the game of hot potato, where anything we don't want to look at within ourself we quickly "throw" to the closest available target.

Special love relationships have the same goal as special hate relationships: to get rid of guilt and shame. The ego simply cleverly disguises the form. In the addictive thought system we think that we are incomplete and needy. We believe that the lacks that we perceive in ourself can never be healed or filled from within. So we begin to search outside of ourself for people or substances that make us feel complete for a period of time. Special love relationships are relationships of conditional love: "If you fill my needs, as I want and expect you to, I will love you. If you fail to do so, my love will quickly turn cold." I feel that this one expectation is responsible for most relationship and family problems.

When I was growing up, my parents showed me mostly unconditional love. I knew that I was important to them, and I received approval for things that I did well. For the most part, their love had a positive effect on my self-esteem. But in some ways their love was conditional; it depended upon my fulfilling specific expectations.

For example, my father's first hour at home was very predictable: home at 6:20 P.M., immediate cocktails with my mother, dinner. At the dinner table the dreaded questions would begin. The questioning would always be in regard to what I had done that day. I always wished that I could say something like, "Well, Dad, after receiving the highest grade on the calculus final in the morning, I went on to throw the touchdown pass at the big game in the afternoon, and was carried off the field on the shoulders of the entire student body." Unfortunately, my answer was usually, "Oh, nothing."

I didn't feel that my dad was asking me because he was really interested, but rather that he was checking up to see if I was deserving of love that day. At the dinner table I never felt that my dad was interested in my true feelings. In fact, I felt that he would not have liked it if I had shared them with him. Had I ever been truthful about my average day, I probably would have said, "Well, Dad, most of the day I walked around comparing myself with other people. I felt self-conscious about how I looked. I felt that I didn't quite belong anywhere, as if I were on the outside looking in. In PE I felt like a geek. I almost threw up while doing laps. We are going to have a test in math this week, and I am going to fake being sick because I don't understand anything and am afraid of failing. After school I smoked a couple of joints with some friends."

I never understood very well what my father did or how he felt. I knew that he was a psychiatrist, but I wasn't really sure what that meant. On a feeling level, I did know that my Dad had two modes. I was aware when my Dad was approving and when he was angry. I saw my job as seeking the approval and avoiding the anger.

As I write this, I am thankful for the healing that has taken place between my parents and myself in my adult years. I can now let them both know how I am feeling at any given time, and feel that they will be accepting of me. Getting to this place with them required that we all take the risks of opening up and being vulnerable. We hadn't really known each other before. Each of us had to choose to share her or his pain in order to let go of it and move to forgiveness. We continue in our process of getting to know each other on deeper levels.

Today, allow yourself to recognize that you are whole within.

Silently, within the depths of your Self,
find all that is perfect and complete.

Open your heart to love
by releasing expectations of yourself and others.

All that you need to know today is that
love is shining in you now.

CHAPTER TWO

The Structure of the Addictive Thought System

You may be beginning to see that it is our thoughts that lead us into pain and addiction, and it is our thoughts that we must heal. *A Course In Miracles* states this beautifully:

> It is your thoughts alone that cause you pain. Nothing external to your mind can hurt or injure you in any way. There is no cause beyond yourself that can reach down and bring oppression. No one but yourself affects you. There is nothing in the world that has the power to make you ill or sad, weak or frail.

There have been endless arguments as to whether such a thing as an addictive personality exists. Though some of us may have a genetic predisposition to chemical addiction, I believe that we are all equally prone to addictive and conflicted ways of thinking which lead to addictive patterns of behavior. We all equally yearn for wholeness and love, and because of this we all may make the mistake of looking outside of ourselves for peace and happiness.

Serenity must come from within. It is my belief that there is only one opposing emotion to love, and that is fear. Fear is something that our egos made up, and fear is at the core of the addictive thought system. Based on fear many other conflicted beliefs occur. I posit that there are four fundamental parts of the addictive thought system. They are fear, living in the past or the future, judgment, and a belief in scarcity. The following diagram illustrates the foundation of the addictive thought system:

The Addictive Thought System

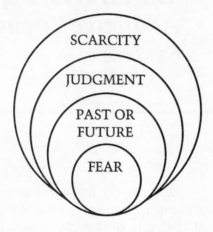

ON FEAR

I have never seen addictive behavior occur where fear was not the driving force.

Fear is the fuel upon which the addictive thought system runs.

Take a moment and think about this statement, for if you are to heal your addictive minds, you must first have an idea of what is at the core of all addictive thoughts and behavior.

Contemplate the following:

When you find yourself looking to a drug, a job, food, material possessions, or a relationship for your happiness, it is because you are afraid, having forgotten that you are love.

When you become like a child, seeing fearsome images in the dark, seeing attack and hostility all around you, your mind has forgotten that you are love, and, in turn, you have become afraid.

When you have an endless résumé of accomplishments and still don't feel good about yourself, love seems to be nowhere and you are afraid.

When you want nothing more than to feel the love of another, yet you continually armor yourself in defenses, it is because you are in an ironic dilemma. You are afraid of that for which you yearn: love.

Projection leads us into a world where fear is constantly reinforced. We end up being afraid of love and freedom. Instead of inviting love into our hearts we become hosts to guilt. We become like captive birds who never learned to fly, sitting in cages surrounded by bars of fear, forged by our own thinking.

Miranda came to see me after she had split up with her husband of eleven years. Miranda had married after becoming pregnant at seventeen. Her father had sexually abused her as a child. She later admitted that she had seen pregnancy and marriage as the only way to get out of her abusive home. Though her mother never physically abused her, Miranda held tremendous anger and resentment toward her for not intervening with her father and providing a safe environment. She was sure that her mother must have known what was going on but remained silent. As a child Miranda learned that it was not safe to talk about feelings in her family so she remained silent, alone with her fears.

Miranda went through her adult life playing out the silent and hidden feelings of her childhood. She always felt as though she were in an unsafe place, and was unable to confide in or rely on anyone. She had few friends and most of her co-workers saw her as distant, defensive, and aloof. Though Miranda wanted closeness with her husband, she felt she could not really trust him, or anyone else. This, combined with her inability to speak of feelings, kept Miranda in a constantly lonely and fearful state.

Miranda came to see me at the request of her employer, because she had been regularly missing work and seemed visibly upset. Miranda, because of her family history, had a difficult time opening up to me. In the course of our early work together, she emerged as a woman who had never felt truly loved. In fact, she had never been told those three simple words: I love you. As a child she had become fearful and mistrusting; as an adult she knew no other way to be.

As our work unfolded, it became clear that there was a part of Miranda that felt guilty for what had occurred with her father. Irrationally, she wondered if she had done something to cause her father's behavior. She also felt guilty because a part of her was thankful to at least have had some attention. The guilt caused her to have many false and negative beliefs about herself. Miranda believed that she was sexually "dirty," and not deserving of a loving relationship with a man. Miranda was longing for love, yet her fear, guilt, and negative self-image kept her stuck in a cycle of either being defensive or isolating herself from others.

You may ask yourself what Miranda's story has to do with addiction. I chose to present Miranda's case because it illustrated the seeds of addiction. Another person could start out with a similar story and go on to use drugs as a way of isolating themself. Yet another could fall into sexual addiction, having many sexual relationships, looking for affection in the only way familiar to them. In Miranda's case she had continued to feel guilty and fearful, which led to isolating and defensive behavior, despite the fact that these behaviors led to continual unhappiness. On a behavioral and feeling level, this was addiction in the sense that she continued to act and think in the same ways despite the adverse consequences. The following diagram illustrates this addictive cycle:

For Miranda this cycle looked like

Miranda was slowly able to trust me and began talking in depth about her feelings, both as a child and as an adult. It took tremendous courage for Miranda to allow herself to break the "no-talk" rule of her family. Miranda joined a support group of women who had been sexually abused and began to see that she was not alone in her feelings of guilt and low self-esteem. This allowed her to open up with other people on a feeling level. As she became less guilt-ridden and fearful, she became less defensive and broke her long history of isolation. Miranda began to experience love in her life. She had never been able to believe in God or a Higher Power, because she had always felt like she would be punished. As she trusted more, she was able to develop her spiritual side. Her heart went from being withered, cold, and isolated to full, welcoming, and open. Several key factors in Miranda's recovery are common to breaking the cycle of fear.

How To Break the Cycle of Fear

1. Begin to talk about your feelings.

This often requires a leap of faith, because many of us think that our feelings are silly, are not worth hearing, or will hurt other people. Others think that what is deep inside is so dark and scary that if we even crack open the door to their existence, we will be overwhelmed. This latter irrational thought is common. In fact, many choose alcohol or other drugs as a means to keeping the door to the darkness of the dungeon sealed shut.

If you do not at first feel comfortable talking to another person, begin by getting a journal and writing down your feelings, including your fears. If you feel that you don't have anyone whom you can talk with, look again. For most people, there really is someone there if we choose to look. Additionally, therapy and self-help groups are a means to start the talking and trusting process.

2. Begin to identify your irrational beliefs, thoughts, and negative self-talk.

The only true statement about yourself is that you are a whole, loving, and fully worthwhile human being. Any statement about yourself that does not reflect this simple truth is an irrational belief about yourself. Any statement other than this keeps you from love and eventually becomes like a weight tied to your ankle.

There is nothing that you have done
in the past that makes you unworthy of love.

There is nothing that you need to do
to become lovable.

This instant you are not only worthy of love,
but you are love itself.

Right now you probably have many irrational beliefs about yourself that are keeping you from experiencing peace of mind. Any unforgiving or condemning thought that you think about yourself locks love out. Begin today to take note of your irrational beliefs about yourself and see the absurdity upon which they rest. Each irrational thought creates a dark and fearful image of yourself and seals the door to love.

3. Begin to see that there is nothing you want to hide, even if you could.

Most of us go through life thinking that there are certain things that we must keep hidden if we want to be loved. We have to bring our fears and dark thoughts up to our full awareness in order to see that they are really based on nothing. Only then can we let them go. It is in releasing our fear that we are healed, not in keeping it hidden.

> The escape from darkness involves two stages: First, the recognition that darkness cannot hide. This step usually entails fear. Second, the recognition that there is nothing you want to hide even if you could. This step brings escape from fear. When you have become willing to hide nothing, you will . . . understand peace and joy. *(ACIM)*

ON LIVING IN THE PAST OR THE FUTURE

What we think time is for and how we use it determines much of what we experience. In the addictive thought system we believe that the past is our stockpile of ammunition to use to condemn both ourselves and others. We constantly think about things that we and others have done "wrong" in the past, and we make "guilt bombs" that repeatedly go off both inside us and around us. Additionally, we hold on to past grievances with other people and end up having anger and resentment eat away at us. Usually even the people with whom we are close do not escape our wrath. We carry around past resentments that become like sandbags, keeping the flow of love out of our relationships. This habit of constantly looking to the past keeps us from knowing who we are.

> Until I direct my mind to let go of the past,
> I will not really know myself and
> love will continue to escape my awareness.

And how does the addictive thought system view the future? The future is a black hole of worry. What better way for the ego to distract us than to create images of catastrophic possibilities that lie in the future!

I would estimate that the average adult spends much more than 50 percent of his or her time preoccupied with something in the future. Questions fill our minds: Will I have enough money to pay the bills? What if I fail? Will this person or that person like and accept me? The list goes on and on. Remember:

Every time we become preoccupied with the future,
we are creating an obstacle for love.
Love lives in the present moment, absent of the past or the future.

Let's look at the past and the future for what they really are.
Quite simply, the past is past: gone, here no more, nonexistent. The
future is not yet here; it exists only in your mind. All of your
worrying is of no use; the ego's sole purpose in prodding you to
worry is to reinforce fear in your mind. In fact, worry can actually
create what it is you are worrying about. This phenomenon is called
a self-fulfilling prophecy.

My grandmother, who died in 1988 at the age of ninety-six,
believed that people could not be fully trusted. She believed that if
she did not keep a watchful eye on people that she would be
cheated, ignored, or treated poorly in some other way. For many
years I saw most of her behavior as moderately paranoid. I knew
that my grandmother loved me very much, and I her, so I went along
with her requests, knowing that it would be of little use to argue
with her.

In her later years she lived in a nice retirement home. On every
occasion that I visited her she would tell me how she was being
treated worse than anyone else, that she was being ignored, and that
she feared that pretty soon she would not be getting any service at
all. I logically assumed that none of this was so, and that it was all
paranoia on my grandmother's part.

One sunny afternoon I was out on my deck, which was beside
a restaurant with outside seating. I was watering some plants when
an intoxicated woman dining at the restaurant tried to engage me
in conversation. At first I tried to just go on watering my plants, but
the woman was insistent. She asked me my name, and I told her, as
I continued to water my plants. When she heard my last name,
Jampolsky, she immediately said, "Ah, shoot, I take care of your
grandma." She was an employee at my grandmother's retirement
home.

"Yeah, I know your grandma," she went on. "She's the biggest
pain in the butt in the place. We draw straws to determine who has
to deal with her that day. She's always suspicious, constantly
thinking that we've stolen something. We all keep waiting for it to

get better, but it only seems to get worse. I can't believe that lady has a normal relative!"

As she droned on, I began to realize that it was not simply paranoia on my grandmother's part. She was, in fact, getting second-class treatment, and it was clear to me why she was.

My grandmother had created for herself what she feared the most. She was so worried about being treated poorly that she was cantankerous and suspicious of everyone. In turn, people avoided her—part of the poor treatment that she had feared. When she was treated poorly, she then had "proof" that she had been right all along and needed to complain even more.

My grandmother, God bless her, taught me a lot about how each person can create his or her own world. If we are projecting a negative future, based on a negative past, chances are pretty good of it happening. The more we become focused on the present, the more we are set free.

> Here in the present is the world set free. For as you let the
> past be lifted and release the future from your ancient fears,
> you find escape and give it to the world. *(ACIM)*

Pain, Time, and Performance

There is nothing about a specific ailment or situation in and of itself that causes us to experience emotional or physical pain. It is our perception, beliefs, and past experiences that determine if we are to feel pain.

Have you ever watched a small child play when his or her parent is nearby? If the child has a minor fall, he or she looks to the parent for a cue as to how to experience this situation. If the parent looks alarmed and runs to the child, the child begins to cry. Alternatively, if, when the child falls, the parent acts like falling is just part of the activity, the child goes on playing.

I have an informal theory about how narcotics relieve pain. When you are under the influence of narcotics, you have a distorted sense of time. Minutes, hours and, with prolonged use, even days, blur together. When this sense of linear time is altered, pain lessens.

A similar phenomenon is seen in many athletes; they can endure prolonged discomfort and still excel in their performances.

Perhaps this is at least partially due to the release of endorphins, an opiatelike substance that the body releases during intense exercise. Many athletes report that during their performances, time takes on a different dimension. The present moment seems to be all that exists. Two examples of this stand out in my mind.

In the 1988 Olympics diver Greg Louganis repeatedly made perfect dives, even after hitting his head on the board during a dive early in the competition. His injury required stitches, but he was back diving the next day. As he stood at the end of the board preparing for his dive, you could feel the intensity of his focused thought. I am quite sure he was not concentrating on the previous day, worrying about hitting his head again, but rather was becoming fully present, in order to perform at his peak. He went on to win yet another gold medal.

I saw Roberto Salazar, a marathon runner, in a newspaper picture a few years ago, leading the pack in about the twenty-first mile. His eyes were half-shut, his breathing seemed normal. His focus was obviously inward. He was not in a state of exhaustion, but rather more in a light trance. Roberto seemed to be inner oriented, away from the linear constraints of time. Crossing the finish line first was simply a result of his ability to be in the present.

There is a direct link between your performance and your perception of time. If you are preoccupied with past failures, there is little chance of you excelling in what you are doing. This is true whether you are an athlete, a businessperson, or a recovering addict. It is also true in relationships. If we are stuck in the past we will never have the relationship that we would like.

ON JUDGMENT

Imagine a world where no one made negative judgments. What a sense of release and total peace would come from meeting yourself and others completely without negative judgment!

> While you are judging, you cannot love.
> While you are loving, you cannot judge.

Think about your own life and all of the times that you have judged yourself or others. Have you ever felt love and judgment at the same time? Look at judgment for what it is and what it creates.

Judgment sentences you to guilt, low self-esteem, and feelings of inadequacy. If you are constantly comparing yourself with others, you can never allow love to set you free.

Judgment and Its Consequences

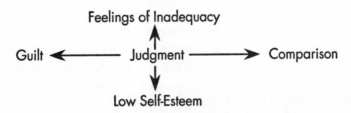

When you look at judgment carefully, you see that whenever you make a negative judgment you are making a choice to experience conflict rather than peace. To understand better how judgment affects your life, imagine that whenever you pass judgment that you are putting on a pair of sunglasses that filters out love.

Many of us have been taught that judgment and analysis are the hallmarks of knowledge and wisdom. Judgment and analysis are indeed useful tools in scientific experiments, but life is not a scientific experiment. And, in fact, even scientists have been finding that reductionism leads to a limited and distorted view of reality. In our personal lives, judgment can hardly be called wisdom. In fact, judgment keeps us from experiencing love. True wisdom lies in the relinquishment of negative judgment, not in the refinement of analytical skills.

With the high rate of divorce, it is painfully apparent that many of us have a problem with the relentless grip of judgment squeezing the joy of love out of our relationships. I went through a divorce myself; that was one of the most difficult periods of my life. Though difficult, my divorce also taught me the effects of negative judgment, especially toward myself.

During my separation my mind seemed as though it were woven in webs of judgment, judgment both toward her and myself. I blamed myself for the divorce, thinking that I had done unforgivable things. At the same time I blamed my ex-wife for not being able to forgive me and commit herself to working on the marriage. This double bind of judgment kept me in pain while enticing my mind to constantly analyze the situation.

I found that the more I analyzed the situation, the more I would compare myself with the ideal husband that I wanted to be. This only led to more self-blame. Self-blame quickly led to anger, toward both of us. This "analyze-compare-blame-anger" cycle only led to increased depression and internal conflict. I came to believe that her decision that the marriage couldn't continue was proof that I was not worthy of love.

I seemed to vacillate between judging her and judging myself. For a short time I was stuck in the mode of judging her. I seemed to believe that if I found fault with her it would relieve my feelings of guilt and self-blame. But judging her was like putting salt on my wound of guilt; it only made my pain worse.

With the help of a therapist I was slowly able to see that I had developed a pattern of sabotaging relationships and then becoming self-critical. I sabotaged my marriage and then used the results as proof that I was "bad" and beyond the possibility of a lasting intimate relationship. Why would I do such a thing as sabotage a good relationship? I was afraid of love and intimacy.

As much as we all want intimacy, many of us are afraid of it, as I was. I am continuing to work on self-acceptance and have become much less fearful of intimacy. By practicing the principles set forth in this book, I have come to more consistently welcome intimacy, instead of running from it. We both learned and grew through the experience of the divorce. Our friendship is very important to me, and I anticipate that we will always see the importance in maintaining it.

The flip side of negative judgment is acceptance and forgiveness. Where judgment builds a wall, keeping love out, forgiveness sends an invitation to love.

> When I have forgiven myself and remembered who I am,
> I will bless everyone and everything I see. (ACIM)

Judgment always sets conditions on love. It says, I will love you if I find you fit my expectations and if you pass my evaluations. A judgmental mind makes lists, often unconsciously, of passing criteria for love. In contrast, forgiveness sets no conditions. Forgiveness simply allows love to be itself.

I invite you to do an exercise to contrast the different experiences that come from judging and from extending love. With your eyes closed, picture someone standing in front of you with whom you are currently experiencing conflict. It may be a parent, a spouse, a co-worker, or even someone whom you have made up. Picturing the person, go ahead and let your mind judge. Let loose all of your judgments. Think of all the negative things that you can about the person. How do you feel as you do this? Most likely you feel anxious, conflicted, and distant.

You can't judge and have peace of mind at the same time.

Now imagine that you have temporary amnesia. Instead of judging this person, see him or her as wanting the same thing that you do: kindness and compassion. Picture the **person** surrounded in a gentle glow of soft white light. Surround him or her with love. If a judgmental thought arises, imagine that it is burned away by the intensity of the loving light surrounding the person. How do you feel as you extend love? My guess is that you feel a sense of release and a sense of peace.

When you extend love, you receive love.

We are always choosing between judgment and acceptance. With practice we can just as easily choose to fill our minds with love-based thoughts as we can the condemnation and judgment of the addictive thought system.

ON SCARCITY

The addictive thought system constantly tells us that we are short on something. Not enough money. Not enough nice possessions. Not enough love. The addictive philosophy of "not enough" stems from one core belief: scarcity. Scarcity is the notion that we are always lacking something. Because of this belief we become caught in endless pursuits to fill this perceived void. We think that our pursuits are valid, yet the following is really happening:

1. Much of our emotional pain comes from thinking that we are lacking, less than whole.
2. The ego tells us to search for things or relationships to make us feel a sense of wholeness.

3. We embark on a search for what we mistakenly think will fill the void.
4. In the end we still feel incomplete. And not knowing any other way to be, we start the process all over again.

The belief in scarcity is so pervasive in our society that we can hardly go through a day without in some way being told that we are not okay as we are. Television commercials tell us that a specific car or a certain kind of coffee or a particular cologne will make us fulfilled and content. We drive down the freeway, full of frustration from demeaning jobs, and see billboards of happy and affluent people smoking cigarettes or relaxing with bourbon. When listening to the news I find that a large percentage of the stories are about people who felt so much like they were "not enough" that they committed crimes out of a sense of desperation and hopelessness.

With such external stimuli it is no wonder that we continue in the mad illusion of thinking that something outside of us will bring us freedom and power. But to think that our feelings of being not enough are the fault of the advertising industry would be naive. What we see in the media is a reflection of our own collective state of mind. When we look into our minds we can see the roots of addiction. I submit that most addictive behavior stems from a three-step process of addictive thinking:

1. I am not okay the way I am. There is a void in me that needs to be filled.
2. There is something or someone external to myself that will fill this void.
3. My happiness is dependent on finding this substance, possession, or person.

In and of itself, this way of thinking can appear to make pretty good sense. The problem with this addictive process is twofold. First, it is based on a premise that simply is not true. The truth is that you are whole and lack nothing in order to be happy right now. Second, the ego's thirst is never quenched. After you buy the perfect TV, you need to buy the perfect car, and then the perfect mate, and so on.

Interestingly, the feeling of yearning for something more is, as discussed in Chapter One, a misdirected spiritual longing. We are like a child who has wandered away from home and gotten lost. All that is on the child's mind is returning home, yet if gone long enough, he or she may forget the faces of his or her parents and the safety of home.

We have wandered away from wholeness and love. In the process we have forgotten who we are and gotten lost. The more we have searched outside of ourselves, the more lost we have become. It is only in the quieting of our minds that we can come to know ourselves.

I worked with Alan, a cocaine addict, when I was directing an outpatient hospital treatment program for chemical dependency. Alan returned for a visit about a year after finishing the program. I knew he was doing fine when he said, "I really appreciate all that you people said to me. But you know, all of our talking would not have kept me clean. Even after stopping the drugs, I still felt like there was something missing. I wasn't sure what it was. One day I just sat down on my bed, shut my eyes, and asked what I was missing. If I had been looking in the window at myself, I would have said that I was nuts. I had never prayed, meditated, or any of that stuff. I didn't hear any words to answer my question, but an overwhelming sense of peace and calm came over me. It was the first time that I recall ever feeling at ease with myself. It was a new feeling, yet it felt ancient at the same time. So what I'm trying to say is, thanks. The talking was important in getting me to look at myself and what I was doing. But it was in the quiet, beyond the words, that I began to find my Self." I knew that Alan had begun to find what he had been yearning for all along: self-love and self-acceptance.

CHAPTER THREE

The Core Beliefs of the Addictive Thought System

The addictive thought system is built upon fear, a past or future orientation, judgment, and a belief in scarcity. The addictive mind becomes bitterly entrenched in this belief system, leaving us devoid of love or serenity.

Addictive Belief Number One: *I am alone in a cruel, harsh, and unforgiving world. I am separate from everybody else.*

If you wake up in the morning and are anything less than joyous about the day that lies ahead, you probably have, to some extent, this belief. The addictive thought system would have us believe that the world is a place full of judgment and separation, and void of forgiveness and union. When we have this belief of separation, we see ourselves pitted against everything in our sight. If you are operating in this belief, it is only logical that you would build walls and defenses to protect yourself. The only problem is that the belief itself is faulty. Herein lies the irrational logic of the addictive thought system: it "logically" reacts to a belief that is not true, yet never wants the belief itself to be questioned.

When we are born into this world, we are fully open, trusting, and without separation. Often experiences in childhood lead us to becoming guarded and untrusting. We begin to develop a belief that we are alone and the world is cruel. As I review my own childhood, I find many of these experiences. Looking back, some are humorous, though at the time they were painful.

One of these tragicomic experiences occurred when I was eight and away at camp. My brother and I were both a bit reluctant to go to camp, but we were also excited about the camp activities and willing to give it all a chance. My first clue as to what was yet to come was the dramatic shift in the counselors' demeanor as my parents pulled out of the parking lot. Fortunately, my brother, who was two years older, became my protector. But even he would be unable to totally shield me from the cruelties of my new world. Before going on, let me give you some useful background.

Fact one: My mother, being attentive to camp rules, had sewn name tags on every piece of clothing that accompanied me to camp. Fact two: My stomach did not accommodate itself well to camp cuisine. Fact three: None of these kids seemed to like me very much. These three aspects of camp life combined forces for the worst two weeks that an eight-year-old could imagine.

One afternoon, following lunch, I received an urgent request from my intestines. I snuck out of archery class and ran to the "outdoor facilities." Unfortunately, I didn't run quite fast enough and I messed my pants. Not knowing what to do in such a predicament, I quickly changed my underwear—and threw the dirty ones in the garbage. What I failed to take into consideration, however, was, first, the mentality of some of my fellow campmates, and, second, the fact that my action would be detected. One kid, a big guy, found my soiled, *monogrammed* skivvies and felt compelled to show them to the rest of the camp population. For the remainder of my stay I was teased relentlessly. To add insult to injury, I had been accidentally hit in the head with a golf club while playing miniature golf. My injury had required a doctor to shave part of my head for stitches. Having a shaved head and being known for pooping in my pants did not make me the most popular kid in camp. Whenever my parents would call to talk to my brother and me, the counselor would stand by the phone and tell us to say that we were having fun. The two weeks were hardly what the camp brochure had promised.

This experience, combined with many more, caused me to build a belief system that convinced me that, in the final analysis, I was alone and unprotected in the world.

From this belief addictive behavior is born. I have come to think that much compulsive behavior is an attempt to avoid feelings of isolation and shame. Rather than questioning the faulty belief, you might be inclined simply to flee from the feelings that it causes. In reversing the addictive thought system you must confront fears of aloneness. Only by doing so can you recognize the truth: that we are all joined and are ultimately more "a part of " than we are "a part from." Think of what a different experience you would have if you always knew that the best way to realize that you were not alone was to extend a compassionate hand to another being. You would never be empty of love again. Think of all of the ways, and the multitude of times, that you have built walls and defenses when all that you needed to do was to think a loving thought or offer a caring touch. In realizing that you always have a choice between building defenses and extending love, your healing begins.

Addictive Belief Number Two: *If I want safety and peace of mind, I must judge others and be quick to defend myself.*

In the addictive thought system a person believes that peace of mind comes from adhering to the following system of insanity:

a. Analyze every person and situation effectively, efficiently, and accurately, relying on your past experiences for information rather than the present.
b. Use your analysis to judge, categorize, and label every person and situation in your life.
c. Get all you can, as quickly as you can, because there is not enough of anything to go around.
d. Attack anything that may threaten you.

Can you see how the preceding limit your life? Every time you analyze, judge, categorize, or defend, chances are good that you are not experiencing love.

Addictive Belief Number Three: *My way is the right way. My perceptions are always factually correct. In order to feel good about myself, I need to be perfect all of the time.*

If I had a dime for every time that I was more attached to being right than I was to being happy, I would be rich.

With this belief (which we may have a hard time admitting to) the individual becomes addicted to being right. Being anything other than right produces feelings of shame. All self-esteem is irrationally based upon being right all of the time. Being less than perfect seems unthinkable.

A large aircraft carrier was at sea. The commander of this vessel, an admiral, was well known for all of his achievements. One night while the admiral was asleep in his quarters, the night watchman saw a light many miles off in the distance. He routinely sent a light signal in morse code, saying, "Approaching vessel, turn ten degrees port [left]." Off from the distance came the reply: "Negative. You turn ten degrees starboard [right]." This presented a problem for the watchman, because the admiral had given orders not to alter course. After the night watchman had tried a couple more times and received the same reply, he reluctantly decided that he should wake the admiral. After being briefed on the situation, the admiral sternly approached the bridge, and, through the signalman, sent the following message: "This is Admiral Smith. I am on an approaching vessel, and I order you to turn ten degrees port." The reply came from the distant light: "This is Seaman First Class Brown. Turn ten degrees starboard." The old admiral, his face flushing with anger that a seaman could be so disrespectful, sent the following message: "This is Admiral Smith of the U.S. Navy. I am commander of the largest aircraft carrier in the world. Turn ten degrees port." The response: "This is Seaman Brown. I am night operator in a lighthouse. Turn ten degrees starboard."

The admiral was addicted to being right. He was sure that he and his crew had assessed the situation properly. He was oblivious to the fact that he was about to run aground, and that Seaman Brown was just trying to offer assistance. I think that all of us have varying degrees of the old admiral's thinking working in our lives. The extent to which we think that we need to be right is the extent to which peace of mind escapes us. When we constantly argue and are attached to being right, we are really arguing for our unhappiness.

Addictive Belief Number Four: *Attack and defense are my only safety.*

The cycle of attack and defense is the vicious cycle by which the addictive thought system sustains itself. If we believe that we are alone in a world where there is not enough to go around, it makes sense to either defend ourselves or lash out in retaliation. Believing that attack and defense are a way to create safety is like throwing a boomerang and thinking that it won't come back. Whenever we attack another, it increases our feelings of being in danger and in need of defense.

Addictive Belief Number Five: *The past and the future are real and need to be constantly evaluated and worried about.*

All addiction has two components: past and future. The addictive thought system is an equal opportunity worrier. The ego worries about all alternatives, thus creating a situation where there is no such thing as a safe future. We feel guilty about our past behavior, and worry either that what it is we are addicted to will not always be there, or that it will always be there. Addictive behavior tends to snowball: it starts out slow and over time becomes so strong that it feels like you cannot live without a certain substance, possession, or person. As the snowball gets bigger it seems that it has a mind of its own and we lose control.

Addictive Belief Number Six: *Guilt is inescapable because the past is real.*

This belief is an extension of the preceding one, but also operates independently. Much of what keeps us from changing our lives is the belief that we have done some acts in the past that are so bad that we must feel guilty. All this belief does is keep us stuck in shame and put a low ceiling on our self-esteem. We feel without hope.

I see this belief at work in many of my recovering (remembering) chemically dependent patients. One patient, Bill, is an alcoholic with seven years of sobriety. In the past seven years Bill has had four sales jobs. In each position he was rapidly promoted, and his employers were all pleased. Despite his successes he never felt good about himself and continued to hope that the next job would be more satisfying. In the course of therapy Bill talked of his career before he became sober. Early in therapy he said that he had worked for one firm for eleven years and that his using alcohol and other drugs had never affected his performance much. His sales figures were always above average and he had never been put on probation. In fact, Bill described his former boss as being one of his best friends. He stated that they had grown up together and were always like brothers. He said that when he first became sober he decided to leave that firm because he thought that he needed more of a challenge.

As our therapy progressed and Bill began to trust me more, he told me something that he had kept inside of himself for twelve years. One cloudy December morning, sitting low in his chair, Bill began sobbing heavily. He covered his face with his hands, attempting to hide the depth of his shame from both of us. Slowly he began to talk. He said that twelve years ago his addiction was costing him more money than he had. He stated that he had also made some bad investments because his judgment was poor while he was using. He then, through his tears, told me that he had embezzled some money from his boss, who was also his best friend, in order to pay his debts and continue his drug use. The amount of money was not large, yet the guilt the act had produced had greatly affected Bill for twelve years. In Bill's eyes he had done something unforgivable, and therefore the guilt was permanent. Quitting that job had had nothing to do with wanting more of a challenge. Guilt had caused him to quit. And something he had done twelve years ago was keeping him from having any satisfaction in the present.

As our work together progressed, Bill became able to forgive himself. Over the years Bill and his ex-boss had grown distant, seeing each other only on occasion. Bill contacted his old friend and told him what he had done and that he wanted to pay the money back. To Bill's astonishment his friend said that he had found out about the embezzlement the year after Bill had left. His friend said that he had been very disappointed at the time, but that he had missed Bill through the years. Bill and his friend are back working together, and Bill has at last let go of his guilt.

Addictive Belief Number Seven: *Mistakes call for judgment and punishment, not correction and learning.*

The addictive thought system is both judge and jailer. When we believe that we should judge and punish ourselves for every mistake, we give ourselves little room to grow. This belief, combined with the belief that "My way is the right way," make a package where internal conflict is inevitable. When we have this belief, every minor mistake we make results in our judging and punishing ourselves. Consequently, we learn little about love.

At one time my wife, Carny, was stuck in a pattern of calling herself stupid. Every time she made a mistake, even a small one, she would say, "How could I be so stupid!" All his did was make her feel badly and lower her self-esteem. She began to realize what she was doing and, with time, was able to catch herself on a more consistent basis. She was able to replace "How could I be so stupid!" with "I'm a human being and we all make mistakes; this is an opportunity for me to learn." As she did this, her self-esteem naturally went up. This allowed her to begin to do things that she had previously hesitated to do, such as return to school.

One negative belief can have pervasive effects on your whole life. One belief can keep you from doing the things you want to do. Reversing just one belief in the addictive thought system can be like waking up to the freshness of a new and sunlit day following a long, dark winter storm.

Addictive Belief Number Eight: *Fear is real. Do not question it.*

The addictive thought system sustains itself with this belief. As long as we don't question fear, the ego stays intact. The ego creates the state of fear in us and keeps us from questioning the illusory foundation on which it stands. If you want to heal your addictive mind, remind yourself of two words: Question fear.

In my work I see some common anxieties that arise from questioning fears. Ironically, fear often increases when we start to look at it. There is the common feeling that if the door is opened to our hidden cellars of fear, we will be overwhelmed. Though fear may increase when we first begin to question the addictive thought system, fear subsides as we recognize its unstable foundation. In fact, examining our fears is likely to result in an overwhelming sense of relief. As we talk about our dark and hidden fears, it usually sheds light and brings recognition of who we really are. Measured to the underlying despair that results from keeping things locked and hidden away, facing our fear is a welcome change.

I currently do a fair amount of public speaking. I enjoy sharing and laughing with groups large and small. Such, however, was not always the case.

When I pursued my bachelor's degree, most of my courses were large enough that I could blend in with the rest of the students and not have to speak in front of the class too often. But whenever I did, my heart would pound so hard it seemed it would pound right out of my chest. I was afraid to speak in front of a group and would avoid it at all costs.

In my first quarter of graduate school, I took a course in ethics that had only twelve students, all of whom appeared to be quite personable. The professor was a kind and soft-spoken man. These facts did not curb my irrational fear of speaking in front of others. I could not blend in and so found myself very uncomfortable. Midway through the class each student had to give a short presentation. My anxiety escalated with each ensuing day. Being ashamed that I was afraid, I kept my fear hidden. The day came and I gave my presentation. I felt horrible during it and the five minutes seemed more like five hours. It was truly a terrifying experience. My anxiety continued as I pondered the thought that I might have to repeat the experience in other classes—how many times I did not even care to speculate. Eventually the fear became so great that I dropped out of school, rather than face giving another presentation.

After leaving school the bottom dropped out of my already low self-esteem. I soon found myself living alone in a remote small town, accelerating my use of drugs. I became withdrawn and reclusive. I never felt more alone.

Eventually I was able to become less isolated, but my fear of letting others see who I was persisted, as did my periodic heavy use of drugs. The fear of being known was really what had fueled my terror of speaking in front of others.

After some time I moved to Seattle, where I later reentered graduate school. I was determined to begin to work through my fear. I chose one very compassionate professor with whom to share my internal struggle. In so doing I took the first step in my healing. Eventually I transferred back to my original graduate school, and spent several years of growth there. Working through my fear was not quick or easy, but making the decision to confront my fear rather than run from it was the turning point for me. I still get a few butterflies speaking in front of others, but I have found that letting others see who I am is the best way for me to get to know myself. Hiding my fears only makes them grow larger, because they begin to feed on themselves.

Addictive Belief Number Nine: *Other people are responsible for how I feel. The situation is the determiner of my experience.*

Here is the core of the ego's blame game. This belief creates a world where you think that peace of mind occurs through luck, not conscious choice. If you find yourself in a favorable situation, we think that we have lucked out and we are happy. If we find ourself in a "bad" situation, we think that we have no choice but to be unhappy. Any time that you say, "If only such-and-such were different, then I could be happy," you are operating in this addictive belief. Realizing this allows you to begin to reverse this addictive behavior.

The only person responsible for how you feel is you.

In the addictive thought system, you tend to blame others and circumstances for your pain and perceived misfortune. This pattern of blaming can become compulsive. I have been told many times by chemically dependent people, "If my marriage (job, car, relationship with my parents, and so on) were better, I would not use." And codependents have often told me, "If only my spouse would change, then I could be happy."

To heal your addictive mind, you must embrace the fact that the situation does *not* determine your experience. Choices are ever present in your life; we but need to learn to recognize them. We each determine what beliefs we want to hold in our mind. And from these beliefs your experience is born.

Addictive Belief Number Ten: *If I am going to make it in this world, I must pit myself against others. Another's loss is my gain.*

With this belief, self-esteem comes from comparing ourselves with others. When we get caught up in comparisons we are always feeling either superior or inferior to others. Either way we lose, because we overlook any sense of union, connection, or togetherness. Think of the "successful" corporate executive who appears to have it all, yet feels alone and without love. Though there are certainly many executives who feel good about themselves, there are also many who are workaholics, and/or alcoholics. Sometimes the loneliness and despair is so strong that the only option that they can see is suicide.

Fortunately, more and more companies are being founded that are based upon mutual cooperation and reinforcing each employee's sense of self-worth, regardless of his or her particular job. These corporations are working on the principle of win/win instead of win/lose. Their goal is to create environments where everybody is treated with respect and dignity.

Union and connection and togetherness are concepts foreign to the addictive thought system. Instead, the addictive mind is in constant battle with its environment, never feeling at ease for any period of time. The addictive thought system defines success in terms of how many bodies you leave in your wake on your way to the top, and how you compare with others.

Addictive Belief Number Eleven: *I need something or someone outside of myself to make me complete and happy.*

Even when we are in the addictive thought system we have the faint underlying feeling that something is amiss, that there must be something more to life than being dragged around by our addictions. Properly perceived, I believe that this feeling is a spiritual thirst, an internal and deep knowing that there is something larger than ourselves. In the addictive thought system this spiritual thirst is repressed. In doing so, an endless addictive pursuit of looking for happiness outside of ourselves is entered into.

As long as we have the belief that we need something or someone else to be whole, we cannot experience true intimacy. We are capable of intimacy when we can enter into relationships knowing of our wholeness and wanting to share openly and honestly who we are. This can't happen when the primary purpose of a relationship is to fill perceived lacks and needs that we think we have.

In the same way, we cannot experience our own feelings and explore our own selves if we are compulsively searching for happiness in possessions, substances, or people. If we are to return to the memory of who we are, we must make the conscious choice to begin to look within ourselves. Until we have the courage to take this step we will continue to deceive ourselves, chasing mirage after mirage and finding only sand.

Addictive Belief Number Twelve: *My self-esteem is based on pleasing you.*

This one belief can cause endless cycles of addictive behavior. "People pleasing" can be an addiction as strong as any drug. In a compulsive quest to please others, we can abandon who we are, losing a sense of self, a sense of identity, apart from pleasing another person. This belief is part of codependency.

It can be confusing: what is people pleasing and what is an act of kindness? The answer depends on your intention and expectations. If you do a deed out of compassion and with a sense of your own wholeness, it is an act of kindness in the light of service. Conversely, if you do the deed because pleasing another is the only way you can feel good about yourself, your attitude will lead you to addiction and despair. In short, it is not necessarily the act that determines whether a person is behaving in a codependent way, it is the motivation and belief behind the act.

Addictive Belief Number Thirteen: *I can control other people's behavior.*

This belief leads us to compulsively trying to control people and situations. Someone with this belief often feels tense, fearing that he or she will lose control. A strong need to control people and situations can lead to ulcers or migraine headaches. The addiction to control can become so intense that the person can never rest or relax.

> The need to control and peace of mind
> can't occur at the same time.

Those who hold this belief often see family members as extensions of themselves; if a child misbehaves or a spouse dresses in bad taste, they take it personally. They want to make sure that family members meet certain standards. But the standards are rarely consistently met, and so embarrassment, shame, and fear become their constant companions. To compensate for these feelings, they might become overly preoccupied with their own achievements.

For those with this belief, only fleeting moments of a thin happiness are possible. If things are going "right," it is only a matter of time before somebody does something that once again points to the fact that they really can't control others' behavior. This only results in a more desperate attempt to control others.

Howard, the husband of a patient of mine, had a compulsive need to control his wife. Janice, his wife, went through an inpatient program for her alcoholism. Howard would not go through the program because he felt that, as a man, he should be able to control his wife. Because he couldn't, he thought this reflected badly upon him. The counseling staff repeatedly tried to meet with him, but he refused. Janice knew that it would challenge her sobriety to return home, yet she decided to do so.

What happened was startling. When Janice returned home Howard immediately locked her in the bedroom. He brought food to her, but would not let her out of the room, because he feared that she would drink again. After four days of this, Janice snuck out of the house at 2:00 A.M., but woke up Howard in the process. She made a run for it, with Howard hot on her trail. The police were called by a neighbor; they intercepted them as Howard was trying to drag Janice back home.

Few would argue that Howard's need to control Janice had become an addiction to the point that he was acting in ways that were totally irrational. But this story illustrates the end stages of the addictive need to control another person in order to feel secure. The seeds to this behavior could probably have been seen fifteen years earlier when Howard would say something like, "Gee, dear, don't you think you have had enough tonight?" In this seemingly benign statement there is still the belief that controlling another person is a possibility, and that we should be able to do it.

The only thing that we are truly in control of is our own thoughts, beliefs, feelings, and behavior. We must give up trying to control other people if we are ever to find happiness.

THE TWO FORMS OF COMMUNICATION

As you were reading about the addictive thought system, you may have felt confused, frustrated or overwhelmed. Perhaps you wondered how you—or maybe someone in your life—could really change.

The addictive thought system is a loud and unrelenting voice. Yet beneath it is the quiet, calm, and ever-present voice of love. Our first step in undoing the addictive thought system is to make an effort to listen to the serene, peaceful voice of love instead of the roar of the ego—the addictive thought system. The intention to listen to love is a powerful tool. Like a river, it will eventually overcome any obstacle.

When you interact with other people operating from the addictive thought system, their defenses and attitudes may make it seem like they are porcupines: when you try to get close, their quills prick you painfully.

Communication can seem very complicated yet it is actually quite simple. It is my belief that there are really only two forms of communication.

The first form is that based on love, where you extend love and compassion to yourself and others. The second form of communication is that based on the addictive thought system; you act defensively, yet deep down yearn for love. In short, the two ways of communicating are 1) extending love, and 2) making a call for love.

Those stuck in the addictive thought system are so afraid that they build walls around themselves. If others attack these walls out of anger, they only reinforce their walls, making them thicker. Taking a jackhammer to addictive behavior does not work: love is the only force that can penetrate the walls of the addictive thought system.

Being loving does not mean being only sweet and nice, tiptoeing around issues that bother you. Stating how you feel, in a loving and nonjudgmental way, allows defenses to quietly crumble. What the addicted person is actually saying is that he or she is scared and in need of love. Nothing less, nothing more. The more we can hear this call for love instead of identifying with the verbal assaults and negative behavior, the greater chance we have of breaking through the walls of addiction.

A process called intervention is a powerful form of loving communication. In an intervention, family members and friends of an addicted person come together, with the help of a counselor, to lovingly and nonjudgmentally confront the addicted person with facts about his or her addiction. Intervention uses love to break through the denial system of the addict. It is my belief that the expression of love never falls upon deaf ears. Love, at the very minimum, begins to open the heart.

CHAPTER FOUR

The Structure of the Love-Based Thought System

From a place of peace, the mind can begin to allow the warmth of love to melt away illusions of fear and guilt. We cannot heal our addictive mind while it is entrenched in fear and conflict. It would be like trying to get out of a Chinese finger puzzle: the harder you pull, the tighter it becomes. Trying to get over fear from a place of fear does not work.

In quiet we begin
to go to the depths of ourself,
finding the memory of love
waiting undisturbed.
Finding love within,
we then begin to share
our fullness with others.

Peace is where love lies waiting,
unharmed by time,
unaffected by the guilt you made
and think is inescapable.
Love is your home,
and it awaits your invitation.

Once you see love within yourself
you will then see it everywhere.
This is because there simply is no place
that you can look where love is not.

It is impossible for your mind to serve two goals at once. For example, I may say that I want peace of mind while still holding a grudge over something that happened last week or last year. If I see any value in holding a grudge, my goal cannot really be peace of mind. Peace of mind is impossible as long as we still see value in the fear-based thinking of the addictive thought system. One purpose of this book is to help you increase your commitment to love. As you begin to want only love, you will begin to see only love. The love-based thought system is just that simple. The only thing that the love-based thought system asks of you is that you lay down the defenses of the addictive thought system and extend the invitation to love. Knowing what you now know about fear, how could you deny this request?

The Love-Based Thought System

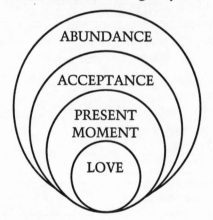

In this chapter the four fundamentals of love-based thinking are discussed, love-based thinking is presented as the peaceful alternative to living in the conflict of addiction.

> If love is sharing, how can you find it except through itself?
> Offer it and it will come to you, because it is drawn to itself.
> But offer attack and love will remain hidden, for it can live
> only in peace. *(ACIM)*

ON LOVE

Many of us grew up in families where the unspoken message was "I'll love you if you do what I want you to do." The "I'll-love-you-if . . ." message causes an individual to think either that he or she is undeserving of love, or else that he or she must please others in order to be loved.

Those of us who received this message began to believe that if we showed our parents all of ourselves, including our dark and hidden thoughts, that we would be rejected. Consequently, we learned to keep certain segments of ourselves hidden, in the hope that we could be fully loved.

Often these messages are covert, and have to do with areas that are either not talked about at all, or are only talked about indirectly. The "I'll-love-you-if . . ." message often relates most directly to sensitive issues, such as sex. With my own family, both of my parents were fairly open about sex, and for this I am grateful. Yet at the same time there were unvoiced expectations about what I would and would not do or be. One such message had to do with homosexuality.

I felt that my mother would be so disappointed that she would die if either my brother or I were homosexual. This was indirectly conveyed to me in myriad ways. Interestingly, my mother had many gay friends and business associates, who were frequently at our house. I was always taught to be accepting of people. I did not feel, however, that this accepting and liberal view extended to my brother or me when it came to sexuality. Though both my brother and I are heterosexual, the following occurred when I was about ten years old. As a result of this experience, I carried hidden guilt and shame for years.

One day a friend and I were wrestling at my house after school. My older brother was a star wrestler, and I looked forward to being the same. As my friend and I wrestled on the floor, we momentarily fondled each other. Both of us were shocked and frightened, and he quickly left for his house. About an hour later my mother came into my room and told me that my friend's mother had called her and was quite upset. I felt immediate despair and shame. Apparently my friend had been so upset that he had told his mother what had happened. My mother asked that I go to his house and apologize to his mother for what had occurred. Full of shame, I did just that.

Standing in front of my friend's mother, I felt like I would never be able to feel good about myself again. I don't remember my mother ever talking about the incident again, but I remember feeling embarrassed and deeply guilty in front of her for some time.

On some level I carried the shame of that experience for about twenty years. Even in graduate school, when I found that such episodes were common, I still kept my experience secret. Somewhere in my mind I believed that because of something that had taken place between two ten-year-old boys, I was not whole. As irrational as it sounds, I was afraid that if people knew my secret, they would see me as deviant and bad. The I'll-love-you-if-your-sexual-behavior-is-what-I-expect message caused me to think that I was undeserving of love.

I might add that in the decades since the incident occurred, my mother has grown at least as much as myself. Today I don't think that she would bat an unaccepting eye should any of her grandchildren reveal to her that he or she was gay.

Most of us have secrets that we keep hidden because we have similar fears. By no means are all of them sexual. Years ago somebody asked me if it were possible, would I be willing to go through one day with a transparent mind. This meant that during a twenty-four-hour period another human being could be aware of my every waking and sleeping thought. At that time this was a frightening thought. I didn't want anybody to know all of what I was thinking for one minute, let alone one day. I was afraid that if people knew my true feelings and thoughts, that I would be rejected in a split second. I believed that if people knew all of what I thought that they would surely see me as angry, hateful, unlovable, and crazy. The extent to which we keep parts of ourselves hidden from all people (and often even ourselves) is the extent to which we are building walls to love.

I am not suggesting that we need to walk around telling every person our most hidden secrets. Rather, I am saying that if we want to experience love, we need to let go of the need to keep parts of who we are hidden, shrouded in darkness, from ourselves and those with whom we would like to be close.

When we feel that we must keep aspects of ourselves hidden in order to be accepted, the result is that we never quite feel deserving of any love and support that we do receive. Groucho Marx once quipped about this feeling, "I wouldn't want to belong to a club that would have me for a member." If we want to undo the addictive thought system, we must begin to realize that we are fully lovable the way we are, because we are love itself.

I enjoy finding fine old wood furniture that has been covered with layers of paint. When I come across a piece, it is not the layers of paint that I concern myself with, it is the beautiful oak, pine, or mahogany that lies beneath the old and cracked paint. As I gently strip off the paint, being careful not to damage the wood, what is beneath is revealed. Stripping off the paint is a long and tedious job. There are times when the wood actually looks worse than when I started, and I am tempted to abandon the project. Sometimes I need to simply have faith that with a little more work I will see the original and beautiful wood. Once the paint is off, I usually need to care for the wood, because it is parched and vulnerable to damp or dry air. After applying a little oil, I end up with a gorgeous piece of furniture.

And so it is with moving from fear to love. Do not concern yourself with the layers of fear and darkness, cracked by years of guilt and judgment. Look beneath and imagine the beauty that waits to be uncovered. Know that it is not necessarily going to be an easy or painless process, but that it will be rich in its rewards. When I am done stripping furniture, I don't go through the scrapings of paint on the floor; I throw them away. They have no use to me. In the same way, let go of your fears. Throw them away like old paint. They have no use to you in love-based thinking.

In the addictive thought system we compulsively search for happiness in people, things, and substances; that process always results in a vicious cycle of fear. In the love-based thought system we look within, going through and beyond fear to find love. As we see love in ourself we begin to see it elsewhere. A child's eyes, a friend's touch, even a group of people we have never met: all become reminders of love. We see love everywhere because it is everywhere. Once love is awakened in our hearts we see that there is no place untouched by love. We can deny the presence of love, but that does not make it disappear. It waits patiently for us to uncover our eyes and open up our heart. When we see darkness and hate, it is like we are seeing old paint on furniture. We always have the choice whether to see darkness or light, in the same way that we can choose to see the paint or the wood.

The first step toward increasing our experience of love is to begin to train our mind to overlook the illusions of darkness—the paint—created by the addictive thought system. Love lies just beyond. Begin to trust in a deeper part of yourself; give it the chance to emerge and be itself. To trust calls for a leap of faith, for fear tells us that if we look within we will not like what we see, and certainly nobody else will. We must begin to trust in our inner life, in our inner guide, for this is the way to uncover the memory of love.

ON THE PRESENT MOMENT

Whenever you are holding onto the past
or worrying about the future,
you are looking nowhere,
seeing things that are not there.

In love-based thinking you go beyond seeing time as linear and instead focus on the present moment. Imagine for a moment how differently you would look upon yourself if you let go of all the past that you use as fuel to feed the fires of guilt and anger. You would see yourself in the purity of the present moment, and what you would see would be love.

Perhaps you have never questioned viewing time in a linear way and consequently participate unthinkingly in a world that is very much ruled by the clock. People seem to be always struggling with time, constantly running to beat the clock. When we first meet another person we may tend to size him or her up in terms of what he or she has done or not done in the past. When we respond to a job advertisement, we send in a résumé: a list of our past. In fact, we may tend to determine our own self-worth by looking at the chronicle of the past that we keep filed in our mind. As a society and as individuals we look to what we have done or haven't done in the past instead of who we are in the present.

When we become focused on the present, the window of our perception radically shifts. We begin to see the world and ourself in a fresh light. There is a sense of newness, release, and relief. There are no outside measuring sticks in the present moment to determine self-esteem; there is only love shining in and around you. As we make this shift in our perception of time, a sense of peace enters into our life.

In my own life I found an addictive pattern of thinking that went like this:

1. When a situation presented itself in my life I would go to my memory banks to determine if this was a "good" or a "bad" situation.
2. If, based on the past, I deemed it good, I would proceed in a fashion that usually resulted in a "positive" experience.
3. If I decided that it was a bad situation, I would become angry, and would always have a "negative" experience.

As I looked at this pattern I began to realize an important fact. I had thought that I was reacting appropriately to each situation, when such was not the case. What I was reacting to was *my perception* of the situation based upon my memory. It had never occurred to me that what I believed the situation to be determined the experience that I had. I found that I could just as easily create a positive experience as a negative one, regardless of the situation. I have come to believe that

> There are no "good" or "bad" situations:
> all situations are simply opportunities to learn.
> What we make of each situation is up to us.

Some years ago I was returning home from a vacation in Mexico. My flight was from Mexico City to San Francisco. At that time the airport in Mexico City had buses that took passengers from the terminals to the airplanes. As I walked to my bus I was preoccupied with my thoughts and not paying much attention to my surroundings, but I was following the signs. I boarded the bus and then boarded the plane. As we taxied out to the runway the flight attendant welcomed the passengers on board the flight, which, she said, was flying to New York via Houston. My jaw dropped. I wanted to go to San Francisco, not New York. For several moments I said the following to myself. (Note how I bounced around from blaming myself and thinking how stupid I was, to blaming others, and finally to worrying about the future, all of which caused shame and embarrassment.)

How could I be so stupid as to get on the wrong plane! I can't believe that I did something like this! This is going to be horrible, just like all of the other times that I have done stupid things. I can't believe that twit of a flight attendant didn't look at my ticket. It is really this incompetent airline that is to blame. Boy, am I going to be embarrassed to have to admit that I got on the wrong plane! People are going to be waiting for me in San Francisco at the airport. I like to look perfect. How am I going to explain this idiotic move?

As you can see, I went to my computer bank of the past and checked for similar experiences. I found these experiences and then ran with them, convincing myself that this too would have a bad outcome.

After my negative self-talk the next thing I did surprised me. I stopped myself and said, "Wait a minute. This doesn't have to be bad." I took a deep breath, shut my eyes, and asked my inner guide to help me change my perception of the situation.

When I opened my eyes I saw that people around me were in a frenzy. Before, I had been so preoccupied with my negative self-talk that I could not even see my surroundings accurately. As it turned out, the bus driver had mistakenly taken us to the wrong plane. I began to laugh, as did the person next to me. We deplaned and were taken to the correct aircraft. As it turned out, the fellow next to me and I had an interesting talk the entire flight. I was able to enjoy myself by letting go and focusing on what was going on in the present moment. When I had looked to the past to determine how I should react, I had seen something that was far from the actual situation. Similarly, when I had worried about the future, I had not even been aware of my seatmate.

I noticed as we transferred planes that people were having basically two experiences. Some were grumbling and angry about the inconvenience, making comments about missed schedules and such matters. Other people, the minority, were seeming to take the situation in stride, as I was learning to choose to do. I began to look at the people who were upset in a different light. I saw that the only difference between peace of mind and conflict was the lens through which a person viewed the situation, and the choice of lens was entirely up to the individual. I was glad that I was learning to choose peace of mind: the present moment. As I learn to accept things that would be impossible for me to change, I find peace of mind.

Peak Performance and the Present Moment

Not too long ago researchers became interested in peak performance. Scientists and psychologists interviewed and observed athletes who seemed to achieve optimal levels of performance. Much of what was learned from these athletes was later applied to nonathletes' lives. And it seems that one thread runs through the ability to reach optimal levels of performance, be it in athletics, relationships, or work:

When we are focused on the present, we move, think, and perform at higher levels than when we are preoccupied with negative thoughts or images of the past or future.

A friend of mine, Dr. Curt Erikson, has been a sports psychologist for Olympic teams. He has had much adventure in his life, including a climb up Mt. Everest. Curt shared with me the following account of an experience he had in the Himalayas:

"In 1985 I had the opportunity to be involved as a sports scientist on a climb in the Himalayas. While camped atop a glacier I, along with my partners, was forced to deal with constant avalanches. Every hour a potentially deadly avalanche presented itself to us. At first there was the temptation to become preoccupied with worrying about the next avalanche. But to worry could kill us, because, combined with the constant stress of altitude sickness, worrying would leave us with no energy for doing what we needed to do. The key to our survival became being focused on exactly what we were doing when we were doing it. Our situation demanded that we stay in the moment. If I focused on the next day, or the previous day, I would be robbed of the necessary energy to keep going. To look to the past or the future would take away from my concentration and alertness, and would make my mind too tired and preoccupied to face any new dangers.

"The evenings and nights were difficult times. Our minds would want to wander, yet we needed to remain alert and attentive to a variety of tasks. In the darkness all of us would struggle with our own demons trying to get the best of us, little chatterboxes of worry that could destroy our ability to concentrate. If I had allowed myself to drift from the 'now' I would have placed myself, and the other members, in great danger. We became a team dedicated to the present moment. We monitored each other and helped each other keep on track. Staying in the moment, was, in a very real sense, a matter of survival. By staying oriented in the present we grew closer, and we all came down the mountain."

There is no greater limit that you can place upon yourself than addictive thoughts. Following are some examples of addictive thoughts. When we think one of these thoughts it produces a negative image in your mind.

1. I can't possibly do this. Nobody has ever before done this.
2. I failed before at this.
3. I have always been bad at this.
4. (*Name*) always said that I would never be able to do this.
5. People are looking over my shoulder; what if I fail?
6. If I make a mistake, it will ruin my whole life.

A number of techniques can help you overcome these thoughts and become oriented in the present. Most of these techniques include the breath in some way.

Watching the Breath

An effective way of becoming focused in the present is to use a simple technique that can be easily practiced, even in times of distress. This technique works best if you are able to close your eyes, though it can certainly be done with your eyes open. Simply bring your attention to your breath: the inflow and the outflow. Begin to watch the rise and fall of your breath, almost as if you were at the ocean watching waves come and go. If your attention wanders at first, gently remind yourself of your task and again focus on the breath. Though your breathing should be natural and unforced, it is helpful to breathe full, deep breaths, filling the chest and the abdominal area.

Some people attach a phrase or affirmation to the breath. This can be something as simple as silently saying on the inhalation, "I am," and, on the exhalation, "relaxed." You can also use a single word, such as *one* or *now*. Experiment to find ways that are useful for you.

The breath has been called the doorway to our inner life. Use of it is certainly a practical and powerful way to let go of your preoccupations with the past and the future. Start out with taking five minutes, three times per day, to practice. Additionally, any time that you find yourself in the addictive thought system, focus on your breath—in the same way that you would take an emergency exit—to get back on track.

ON ACCEPTANCE

The basic tenet of the addictive thought system is judgment: the belief that constantly analyzing, comparing, criticizing, and condemning are traits that bring security and peace. In contrast, the love-based thought system sees that peace of mind is obtained through the art of practicing acceptance.

In much of clinical training there were certain assumptions made by clinicians that were rarely questioned. For one, there was an assumption that the individuals who came seeking treatment were having some problems in certain areas of their life and that they desired change. We saw ourselves as "agents of change" and would try to help change the patient to a "higher functioning" person. I do not question that most, if not all, people in some way want change; I am positing that there may be more than meets the eye in how we achieve change.

I have come to see that a certain phenomenon must occur before deep change—that is, change that occurs on both the behavioral level and the feeling level—can occur. I call this phenomenon the paradox of change.

In order to truly change, we must first accept ourself just as we are, without reservation. We must be able to see beyond our dysfunction and see our essential wholeness. If we do not approach ourself with an attitude of acceptance and love, we beat ourself up. And as long as we beat ourself up, positive deep change is impossible. The only change that occurs by condemning yourself is that you end up feeling worse about yourself.

Paul came to see me following a separation from his wife. Paul, a construction supervisor, had previously identified strongly with the image he had of himself as a family man. He stated that he was having a hard time adjusting to the separation and that he was often depressed. In the first two months that he was seeing me, he dated several women. He would have a week or two of heavy romance with a woman, break up with her, and then feel empty and think that nobody could ever replace his wife. Paul began to see that he could come to our sessions and talk openly about what was going on in his inner life without feeling negatively judged by me. And because I did not judge him negatively, Paul began to judge himself less harshly. Slowly he opened up.

Paul began to realize that his relationship with his wife had actually never been good. In fact, throughout his seven-year marriage he had almost always felt the same emptiness that he was then experiencing. Finally, after several months, Paul was able to share with me that as a child he had been molested by a male relative, over a period of years. In discussing this he was then able to discuss his deeply hidden fear that he might be homosexual. Paul had had several homosexual experiences as an adult and felt tremendous guilt as a result.

Paul began to explore the issues surrounding his molestation and his questions about his sexuality. During this time my primary task was to extend acceptance to Paul. If Paul could begin to feel accepted for who he was, he could then explore these issues without being so full of shame. Paul could not make change without first feeling accepted.

> The paradox of change is that we can't effect deep change until we first accept ourself just as we are.

To my mind the various twelve-step self-help groups, such as Alcoholics Anonymous, work not so much because of what is said during the meetings, but because of their attitude of acceptance. The attitude is, "We accept you as you are today, and should you want to look at various aspects of your life, we're here to help you through it with love, without judgment."

Here are a few thoughts about the nature of acceptance of yourself and of others:

1. Our energy is exhausted when we judge, analyze, compare, and criticize. Conversely, we feel enlivened when we extend acceptance.
2. Peace of mind comes from accepting who we are rather than evaluating and punishing ourself for what we have done. Likewise, peace of mind also comes from accepting others.
3. Acceptance is based on the present moment. Judgment is based on the past.

4. Acceptance does not mean condoning negative behavior. It simply means that to change our own negative behavior (or to encourage another to change) we must see that there is a worthwhile person beneath the behavior.
5. Peace of mind comes from accepting things that are not within our power to change. This means recognizing that we cannot control other people.
6. Acceptance does not know anything about expectations. Acceptance is not attached to future outcomes.

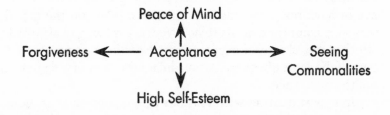

Where judgment makes love conditional,
acceptance allows love to be itself.

Judgment sets criteria for love.
Acceptance sets none.

In judgment we become constricted, rigid, and fearful.
In acceptance we become open, fluid, and loving.

Let me suggest an experiment that you can conduct to illustrate for yourself, on a feeling level, the difference between acceptance and judgment. Take two hours of your day. In the first hour, the hour of judgment, be very concerned with the past, especially regarding what people have or have not done for you. Be as judgmental as you can, passing judgment on everybody who crosses your path. Mentally criticize yourself and others mercilessly. Don't act upon your critical thoughts. Just pay attention to how you feel while you are thinking judgmental thoughts. Do you feel good about yourself? Do you feel close to other people? Do you feel at ease? Or are you scared and uptight?

During the second hour, switch to an hour of acceptance. Begin by practicing a few minutes of the breathing exercise presented earlier in this chapter. See the inner glow of love in people, even if it is just a faint flicker deep beneath the surface. If you have a particularly hard time seeing the love in someone, imagine what kinds of events must have occurred in his or her life that would lead to his or her current behavior; understand how much he or she yearns for love. Look beyond behavior and see the whole person. Imagine that you were born just today, this hour, that everything is fresh and new. Don't be concerned with what you or other people have or have not done. Instead, choose to focus on the fact that everybody wants and needs to be loved, accepted, and affirmed for who they are, absent of expectations. Now how do you feel? Ask yourself the same questions as you did for the hour of judgment and note the difference.

In experimenting with an hour of judgment and an hour of acceptance, you begin to learn that you really do choose the thought system in which you operate. Whether you extend judgment or acceptance is a choice that only you can make. And, consciously or unconsciously, it is a choice that you make every minute of every day. You can just as easily choose one as the other. I hope that you will begin to choose acceptance with increasing frequency.

ON ABUNDANCE

Even though we may not remember them well, I believe that all of us have had moments in our lives where we felt complete and fulfilled, moments where there was no perception of lack, only wholeness and love. In these moments we spontaneously break through the confines of the ego's belief in scarcity and become aware of the truth of who we are.

We can bring these spontaneous breakthroughs under conscious control by being absolutely clear about what it is that we want.

Peace of mind is what I want.
This very moment I am full of love.

How could I not receive what I want
when I ask for what I already have.

One winter day a few years ago I found myself burdened with problems. I felt as though I was locked into a life that was not how I wanted it to be. If I had made a list of what I thought I needed to do before I could breathe easily, it would have been quite a long list. It was a shadowy, misty day, and that seemed to only add to my depression. I was driving to work, preoccupied with all that I thought I had to do, when an unusual idea broke through my thoughts: drive over to the beach. I had a busy day ahead of me and ordinarily would have ignored such a thought. But that day was different; I decided to go. When I got there I sat on the damp rocks edging the bay and looked out over the water. Instead of thinking of all I had to do, I allowed the beauty of the winter morning in. All of a sudden there was a dramatic shift in my perception. All the thoughts of things I had to do gave way to feelings of completeness in the moment. A healing awareness came over me. There was nothing that I had to do in that moment other than be exactly where I was, experiencing exactly what I was experiencing. I felt full of life and love, and knew, as I sat on the rocks, that I needed to accomplish nothing else in order to have peace. All that I needed to do was to allow what was already there to come through. It was as if the sun had come blazing through the winter sky. In a moment's time I had shifted from thinking that it was impossible for me to be happy under the given circumstances to realizing that I could shift my perception and experience the freedom of the present moment.

The ego tells us that we live in a world where our happiness depends upon getting more. It tells us that how we get more is by doing more. The problem is that the addictive thought system has the philosophy of What You Have Is Never Enough. Once we have what we think we need, then our energy goes into guarding what we have and getting more.

The love-based thought system recognizes that the ego's thought system is insane, and only leads us into conflict. Abundance is the simple recognition that what is of value does not decrease in value over time, and does not need to be guarded. What is of value grows in value when it is given away. When we embrace abundance we determine what is valuable in a completely different way than when we view the world through the lens of scarcity.

1. The true test of something's value is whether it increases when it is given away. For example, love, kindness, compassion, and caring all increase when shared with others.
2. Time does not diminish what is of value.
3. The addictive thought system says, "I must do something else before I can have peace." The love-based thought system says, "In a quiet mind peace becomes known."
4. What is of value needs no defense; peace comes to those who offer peace.
5. Love is drawn to itself. Attack is drawn to itself. What you value is what you choose, and the choice you make determines everything.
6. The key to peace is to give to others what you already have, instead of trying to get what you think you need.
7. Abundance offers escape from the thought that you are not enough through a recognition that you are everything.
8. Abundance sees no value in fear, because abundance recognizes that there is nothing of value that can be lost.
9. When you know that you have love, and are loved, what else would you want to do but share what you have.
10. Abundance values win/win situations. The ego values win/lose situations.

It may sound like abundance suggests that people stop work or do nothing. This is not true.

I had the good fortune to spend some time with one of the great teachers of abundance: Mother Teresa. She certainly can't be accused of doing nothing. And, at the same time, when she starts up a mission she doesn't think in terms of scarcity, saying, "Oh, we can't do this because there is not enough money." Mother Teresa knows that loving and kindness are all that is truly important, and that all else falls into place from this. It is not a pretty room or fancy food that creates healing; it is love. Mother Teresa certainly works very hard, but she is working from the place of abundance, knowing what she has to give; not scarcity, wondering what she will lose.

The love-based thought system—which includes an attitude of abundance—can truly heal the addictive mind.

The ego sees problems and obstacles in every situation.
Love-based thinking sees opportunities to learn in every situation.

Addictive thinking holds onto fear, irrationally
believing that fear serves some use.
Love-based thinking recognizes that healing is releasing fear.

Addictive thinking holds onto the negative past, thinking that
grudges and guilt serve a purpose.
Love-based thinking sees that healing is letting go of the past.

The ego tells you that seeing lack, fault, or unworthiness in
someone else makes us feel all the more powerful.
Love-based thinking states that healing is recognizing the worth in
everything and everybody.

The ego equates *judging* yourself with healing yourself.
Love-based thinking equates *loving* yourself with healing yourself.

The addictive mind tells you that you are separate and that your
thoughts don't make a difference.
Love-based thinking tells you that the most powerful healing force
is a loving and forgiving thought that joins everyone.

CHAPTER FIVE

The Core Beliefs of the Love-Based Thought System

The love-based thought system is built upon love, the present moment, acceptance, and abundance. Beliefs based upon this thought system bring peace of mind.

Love-Based Belief Number One: *What I see in others is a reflection of my own state of mind. There is an underlying unity to all life. I lack nothing to be happy and whole right now.*

This three-part belief begins by affirming that what we see in the world is our own state of mind projected outward. In other words, we are always looking through a filter of our own thoughts and beliefs. And, as discussed earlier, the thought system in which we operate determines how we see other people and situations. In the addictive thought system we constantly blame others, seeing a world that is against us. The love-based thought system has no beliefs that support the blame game.

The second part of this belief is the recognition that we are not detached from each other, but are, in fact, connected by the thread of love.

It would be hard to imagine a more isolating existence than being a prisoner of war (POW) in solitary confinement. While in solitary many POWs lost their will to live and some lost their sanity. Yet others survived the experience intact. Accounts by those who survived suggest that they had one thing in common:

71

they were able to realize that they, despite their solitude, were not alone. Some thought about their families and sent them love, and felt the love that their families were sending them. They did not see the confines of their cell as able to keep love from them. They survived by understanding that love knows no boundaries.

Other POWs survived by mentally connecting with the other prisoners of war. They would silently send the others strength and compassion throughout the day, and understood that others were doing the same for them. They could feel the strength of other prisoners lifting them above their despair.

Still other POWs got through the experience by deepening their relationship with God. They were able, through prayer and meditation, to know that they were not alone.

It is my belief that the prisoners who developed severe emotional problems and lost all sense of purpose and hope were the ones who believed that they became alone when the cell door shut. The experiences of the survivors show us that the strength of the human spirit lies in the knowledge that we are intimately and deeply connected. Love never abandons us. It is we who can choose to abandon love.

The third part of this belief speaks to the fact that we are whole and without lack at this very moment. This knowledge allows us to turn to the love within instead of thinking that we must do something more before we can be happy.

Love-Based Belief Number Two: *My safety lies in my defenselessness, because love needs no defense. Acceptance is what brings me peace of mind.*

The ego tells us that our defenses will make us feel secure, yet all that results are increased feelings of isolation and fear. It is impossible to feel secure while we are building high walls behind which to hide. Safety and security are by-products of peace of mind. In laying down our defenses and adopting an attitude of acceptance our world changes.

Beth and Bob had been married for four years when they came to see me. Both had been married previously and had gone through bitter divorces. When the behavior of one spouse reminded the other in some way of the former marriage, the spouse who felt threatened would quickly raise his or her defenses. This would then make the other person equally defensive.

Each secretly feared that this marriage would end up like their former marriages. This fear led each of them to put up defenses whenever he or she thought that this fear was coming true.

Beth and Bob each began to see that when they acted defensively, this led to them feeling insecure, afraid, and distant from each other. Over a few months they learned that they could just as easily drop their defensive stances and talk with each other about their fears. They found that becoming less defensive and more communicative resulted in increased closeness and allowed them to feel a greater sense of security in the marriage.

In laying down their defenses, they found that they were more self-accepting and more accepting of each other. When they had feared that this marriage would end up like their former marriages, they constantly looked for evidence to confirm this hypothesis. In talking about their fears, instead of defending against them, they felt safer in the relationship and they began to know each other better. In the course of their conversations they also brought up the issue of leftover guilt about how they had behaved in their previous marriages. In talking to each other they helped each other let go of this secret guilt.

Love-Based Belief Number Three: *My self-worth is not based upon my performance. Love is unconditional.*

As children many of us learned that when we performed well we received praise. In families where performance was seen as extremely important, the children grew up feeling like anything short of perfection meant that they had failed. And, in fact, even attaining a high goal meant, at the most, only momentary satisfaction. The children learned that no matter what they did, it was not quite sufficient.

When we believe that our self-worth is based upon our performance, we invariably end up with feelings of inadequacy.

Suzy grew up in a family where perfect performance was the only way to get positive attention from her parents. If Suzy received five As and one B+, her parents would ask, "Why didn't you get straight As?" Suzy went to college on a number of academic scholarships. Despite her "success" she often would wake up with her stomach in such a knot that she had to vomit. She feared receiving any grade less than an A, anything less than perfect. As an adult Suzy kept up her pattern of overachieving and became an executive in a large company at age twenty-seven. But Suzy still didn't feel good about herself and was plagued by her continued fear of failure.

Brian grew up in a family similar to Suzy's, but he adopted a different way of compensating. Brian did poorly in school, never went to college, and ended up in a menial job. He never put out much effort despite the fact that he was very bright. At an early age, as a result of his parents' constant dissatisfaction, Brian adopted the attitude of "No matter what I do, it is not good enough, so why bother? If I never try, I will never have to fail."

The common thread between Suzy and Brian was their belief that their performance determined their worth as human beings. The task for both of them was to let go of this addictive belief. To end the addictive cycle of behavior they needed to recognize that the love we receive and our self-worth are not based on what we do.

We were all born into this world fully worthwhile and lovable, and without shame. It is our task to get back in touch with this core of who we are.

Love-Based Belief Number Four: *Forgiveness, with no exceptions, ensures peace.*

Albert Einstein once suggested, in reference to the nuclear bomb, that if we are to survive the nuclear age our thinking must change. I believe this to be true in interpersonal relationships as well as international ones. Defense and attack are ways of thinking that have become normal for many of us. Our world seems to collectively believe so much in defense and attack as a means to safety that we "normally" kill hundreds of thousands of our fellow human beings every decade.

If we want safety and peace, be it on an interpersonal or an international level, we must change our way of thinking by beginning to forgive, rather than defend and attack. Forgiveness is the subtle shift in our perception that allows us to see our commonalities instead of our differences. Forgiveness is a warm and gentle rain, washing away our negative view of the past.

A few years back my father, Jerry Jampolsky, and Diane Cirincione cofounded a group called Children as Teachers of Peace. They saw that children were often more accomplished in the art of forgiveness than adults. Though children often have disagreements, they seldom last long. Usually they are able to overlook or forget the conflict and get back to what is important: playing together. And when major disagreements do arise between children, they don't consider killing large numbers of people to solve their individual differences. Think of how we all might benefit from the teachings of our children.

Ask yourself honestly: When has defense and attack ever brought me peace of mind? Assuming that you want peace of mind, begin to see the value in forgiveness.

> *What could you want*
> *forgiveness cannot give?*
> *Do you want peace? Forgiveness offers it.*
> *Do you want happiness, a quiet mind,*
> *a certainty of purpose,*
> *and a sense of worth and beauty*
> *that transcends the world?*
> *Do you want care and safety,*
> *and the warmth of sure protection always?*
> *Do you want a quietness that cannot be disturbed,*
> *a gentleness that never can be hurt,*
> *a deep, abiding comfort,*
> *and a rest so perfect it can never be upset?*
> *All this forgiveness offers you.*
> *(ACIM)*

Love-Based Belief Number Five: *Only the present is real. The past is over and the future is not yet here.*

Embracing this one thought opens the door to love and closes the door to fear and worry.

I lived much of my life worrying about the future. I used to wake up in the morning worrying about the day ahead. And I would go to sleep worrying that tomorrow might be worse. During the day I would critique my performance and wonder what I could have done differently.

Many of us have this habit. For example, I see this thinking pattern of worry-critique-worry in my college students on the first day of class.

On the first day of class I ask the students to introduce themselves, say a little about their personal interests in the particular course, and add anything else that they wish. The seating is usually in a large semicircle and the students start at one end and proceed to the other. In observing the students I have noticed that the closer an individual comes to his or her turn to speak, the less that person listens to what is being said by his or her classmate. The student seems to be busy mentally rehearsing what he or she is going to say. Then after the student speaks he or she is still not fully attentive: the person seems to be critiquing his or her performance. And after the introductions are over, a student's attention may turn to worrying about whether he or she will need to speak in class again. With all of this mental activity there was not much time left over to pay attention to what was really happening in the present moment.

It is easy to fall into this way of thinking and end up missing much of what is going on in our lives because we are so involved in the addictive cycle of worrying, rehearsing and categorizing.

Love-based thinking brings our focus back to the now. When we focus on the present, life takes on newness and stress is greatly reduced. It is my belief that most stress-related illness is caused by preoccupation with the past and the future. I would therefore say that for optimal health, we need to be oriented to the present.

Love-Based Belief Number Six: *In order for me to change my experience, I must first change my thoughts.*

It is our thoughts, our attitudes, that need healing if we are to find happiness. In love-based thinking we pay attention to our thoughts and attitudes rather than spending our time complaining, judging, finding fault, and being afraid.

Every situation that arises gives us the opportunity to learn of love.

We often invent elaborate ways of avoiding our feelings of guilt. Most often these ways are some form of the blame game, where we think that we can make our guilt smaller by making others' guilt bigger. Love-based thinking sees guilt for what it is: a condition where the addictive mind believes that there is something that we have done that we should always punish ourselves for. Forgiveness, the peaceful alternative to guilt, is a state of mind that recognizes that we are reborn in each new moment, and that the light of love can be covered up, but never extinguished. In love-based thinking we simply recognize the choices that we have.

Love-Based Belief Number Seven: *Mistakes call for correction and learning, not judgment and punishment.*

Many people grew up in families where making a mistake was treated as though they had just let the world down. The parents in such families do not often praise and affirm the children, but instead seem to be always on the lookout to find fault and punish. Usually, the parents behave this way because they think that the children will learn best by being told what *not* to do.

Chuck, a twenty-eight-year-old man, came to see me a few years ago, following a divorce from his wife. Chuck had a beautiful four-year-old son; his wife had custody of him. Chuck said that he had had the perfect marriage and had thrown it away when he thought he was in love with another woman. He had left his marriage, only to find out that the new woman in his life did not want to be with him after all.

Chuck's father had always been controlling and critical of Chuck. When his father had found out what Chuck had done, he had told him that he was stupid, that he only wanted sex from this new woman, and that he would never amount to anything. His father, at the top of his lungs, had then told Chuck that he was disowning him, and never wanted to see him again. Chuck, as always, felt full of shame upon hearing his father's words, and was unable to let go of it. At the time Chuck came to see me this had all happened one year before, yet he was still punishing himself. He had become his own critical parent. And as long as he continued to punish himself he stayed stuck in shame.

Chuck was slowly able to see that leaving his wife was a situation that had occurred that called for learning, not punishment. Chuck was able to begin to explore the fears that he had had in his marriage that had lead up to his action. Though Chuck's father did not allow contact between them, insisting on continuing to punish him, Chuck was able to see this as being about his father, not about him.

Chuck got in touch with the lonely child deep within himself. Instead of always assuming the role of critical parent when it came to himself, Chuck began to be able to nurture and love this child within. As he did this he was able to accept what he had done without the need to punish himself. Punishment had kept him shackled to the past; with love he was able to learn and move on.

The only limits to our learning
are ones that we make up.

Our minds are limitless
in their ability to learn of love.
Creative power is set free when we release ourselves
from the confines of self-criticism.

Love-Based Belief Number Eight: *Only love is real. And what is real cannot be threatened.*

In the addictive thought system we always feel threatened. It is impossible to feel threatened and have peace of mind at the same time. The love-based thought system recognizes that the addictive thought system is a world of illusion based upon faulty beliefs. Unconditional love has no enemy, no fear of being destroyed: it is everywhere and all that is. There is nothing to oppose love and no need for defense.

Love-Based Belief Number Nine: *I am responsible for the world I see, and I choose the feelings that I experience. I decide upon the goal I would achieve.*

With this belief we give up blaming others and begin to take responsibility for our own lives. When we have peace of mind as our single goal, that is what we will achieve.

Instructors of criminology often use a dramatic example to demonstrate to the students how each person sees things through his or her own perception. A class of thirty people will be shown a film of a crime being committed. The students will then be asked to write down what they saw. They are asked what their opinion is regarding why the crime was committed, who the victims are, and who the suspects are.

The instructor usually receives back thirty different responses. Even the seemingly obvious facts, such as hair color and the weather, are rarely all the same. This illustrates that each person sees the world through his or her own filter, coming to different conclusions from the same information.

If we look through green glasses we see a green world; if we look through rose glasses we see a rose world. Seeing the world through the addictive thought system we see a world that calls for us to defend and attack. Seeing the world through the love-based thought system we see a world that calls for us to extend love and compassion. We see two different worlds, and have two different sets of experiences, depending upon which thought system we use.

A friend told me the story of how a burglar broke into his New York apartment while he was sleeping. He said that he was awakened in the middle of the night by sounds in his living room. When he went into the living room he was met by a very nervous burglar, who yelled at my friend to get back in his room and shut the door. My friend's first response was fight or flight: he was either going to run or he was going to confront the man. But instead of one of these responses my friend, surprising himself, chose not to see this young, frightened burglar as an enemy, and he began to talk to him. He told the burglar that he had little attachment to his possessions and that he was free to take what he needed. He even asked the man if there was anything that he needed, and if he was hungry. You can imagine the confused look on the burglar's face. After a few moments the burglar began to be less defensive and hostile, and even became less nervous. The burglar ended up apologizing to my friend, and told him that he had been homeless for some time and was feeling desperate. He said that this was the first burglary that he had ever committed. My friend began consciously to extend compassion to this lost and homeless person standing in front of him. Then my friend surprised himself further. He said that he would like to offer him some money to get a meal and a place to stay for a few days. The astonished burglar accepted, and left my friend's possessions where they were. The burglar and my friend shook hands, and the burglar left through the front door, instead of the window through which he had entered. Who knows what happened to that man. But I am sure that he left that apartment feeling loved. My friend said that he could not have responded as he did until he became aware of how he could choose between fear and love. This was graphic proof for my friend that he does in fact choose the feelings that he experiences and the goals that he achieves.

In any situation it can be helpful to ask yourself this simple and straightforward questions: What do I want to come of this? What is the purpose of this situation?

Many times we do not adequately clarify our goal—to learn of some aspect of love—at the beginning of a situation. When we do not clarify our goal we are inviting the addictive thought system to run wild, creating dust clouds of conflict.

Love-Based Belief Number Ten: *To give is to receive. For me to gain, nobody can lose.*

We all yearn for the quiet calm of peace of mind. It is through centered giving that we find peace of mind. The equation is simple:

> To have peace, give peace.
> To know love, offer love.

Centered giving is giving from a place of knowing that we are whole and complete, and wanting to share with others. This is in contrast with codependency, where we feel that our self-esteem is dependent upon caring for others.

In love-based thinking there is no concept of losing. Love does not keep itself from some while shining on others. When we think that we lack in some way, we are listening to the voice of the ego.

> Peace of mind is found through sharing and joining,
> not selfishness and separation.

Love-Based Belief Number Eleven: *I am complete right now.*

When we begin to believe this, all the various forms of seeking outside of ourselves for happiness cease. When we realize that we already have what we are looking for, we feel relief, and also amusement at our silliness.

Sometimes I will run around my house looking for the keys to my car. I'll turn things over, ask my wife where they are, and work myself into a frenzy. Then I will reach into my pocket (the same pocket that I had looked in before) and find my keys. My wife has a special look that she reserves for this situation.

When we begin to practice love-based thinking we have a similar experience, but on a spiritual level: all of a sudden we find that love and serenity have been available to us all along. We had been so busy looking outside of ourselves that it had not occurred to us to become quiet and look within.

Love-Based Belief Number Twelve: *My self-esteem comes from loving and accepting myself as I am today, and then sharing love and acceptance with others.*

If we have feelings of low self-worth we may try to become "people pleasers," thinking that if we make everybody feel good, then we will feel better about ourselves. The problem is that we end up never feeling comfortable with ourselves unless we are trying to please others.

We cannot truly love and accept others without first loving and accepting ourselves. When we try to be people pleasers, it is as if we are trying to fill a hole with dirt from another hole; we still have a hole. The first step toward loving ourselves—reducing our people-pleasing efforts—may be the hardest. This is because when we stop people pleasing we are left to face the real feelings that are beneath the behavior.

Remember, stopping the addictive thought system often leads to a time of despair. That is how addictive thinking keeps itself going: by telling us to be afraid of love and telling us that we need elaborate defenses.

Love-Based Belief Number Thirteen: *I can't change others, but I can change how I perceive others.*

This is simply a statement revealing that we know what power we have and what power we don't have. When others engage in behavior that we dislike, the primary thing that we can do for our own peace of mind is to extend compassion and love to them. This is an outrage to the addictive thought system: the ego tells us that the primary thing that we should do is change them.

Love-based thinking does not mean that we should not say how we feel, not speak out about cruel, violent, or oppressive behavior. It simply says that our *primary* task is to extend love.

Let us imagine a father and his seven-year-old son. The son has just been sent home from school because he has been picking fights with the other children. The behavior is obviously not in anyone's best interest, but what is the real need of the child? Should the father only punish his son, seeing his primary task as trying to change his behavior? Or would it be more appropriate for him to perceive the child's behavior as a call for love that is stating that the child is in internal conflict in some way? Should the father's primary response be out of love and compassion, or out of anger and the desire to change his son? Responding in love does not mean that the father should condone the child's behavior; in fact, some consequences might be in order should the behavior continue. But regardless of the consequences, love-based thinking would respond with the attitude of love, caring, and the desire to understand.

This attitude is in no way limited to parenting children. If our primary goal is to change others, chances are that we are in the addictive thought system. If our primary goal is to love, care, understand, and communicate, chances are that we are in the love-based thought system.

COMPARISON OF THE ADDICTIVE THOUGHT SYSTEM AND THE LOVE-BASED THOUGHT SYSTEM

In this chapter the core beliefs of the love-based thought system have been presented; the core beliefs of the addictive thought system were presented in Chapter Three. On the next two pages you will find a side-by-side comparison of the two thought systems. Refer to these lists when you find yourself caught in addictive thinking. Identify which of the addictive beliefs you are primarily operating under, and then look across to the corresponding love-based belief. Knowing the corresponding belief will help you to see your choices. It gives you the opportunity to change your mind.

By itself positive thinking does not necessarily bring about change. You must also identify the negative belief—the addictive belief—that is keeping you from being able to embrace the truth. Thus, if you find yourself in conflict, your first task is to identify the addictive belief. Your second task is to replace it with love-based thinking.

BELIEFS OF THE ADDICTIVE THOUGHT SYSTEM

1. I am alone in a cruel, harsh, and unforgiving world. I am separate from everybody else.
2. If I want safety and peace of mind, I must judge others and be quick to defend myself.
3. My way is the right way. My perceptions are always factually correct. In order to feel good about myself, I need to be perfect all of the time.
4. Attack and defense are my only safety.
5. The past and the future are real and need to be constantly evaluated and worried about.
6. Guilt is inescapable because the past is real.
7. Mistakes call for judgment and punishment, not correction and learning.
8. Fear is real. Do not question it.
9. Other people are responsible for how I feel. The situation is the determiner of my experience.
10. If I am going to make it in this world, I must pit myself against others. Another's loss is my gain.
11. I need something or someone outside of myself to make me complete.
12. My self-esteem is based on pleasing you.
13. I can control other people's behavior.

BELIEFS OF THE LOVE-BASED THOUGHT SYSTEM

1. What I see in others is a reflection of my own state of mind. There is an underlying unity to all life. I lack nothing to be happy and whole right now.
2. My safety lies in my defenselessness, because love needs no defense. Acceptance is what brings me peace of mind.
3. My self-worth is not based upon my performance. Love is unconditional.
4. Forgiveness, with no exceptions, ensures peace.
5. Only the present is real. The past is over and the future is not yet here.
6. In order for me to change my experience, I must first change my thoughts.
7. Mistakes call for correction and learning, not judgment and punishment.
8. Only love is real. And what is real cannot be threatened.
9. I am responsible for the world I see, and I choose the feelings that I experience. I decide upon the goal I would achieve.
10. To give is to receive. For me to gain, nobody can lose.
11. I am complete right now.
12. My self-esteem comes from loving and accepting myself as I am today, and then sharing love and acceptance with others.
13. I can't change others, but I can change how I perceive others.

CHAPTER SIX

Addiction and the Fear of Intimacy

When I first began working in the field of chemical dependency most counseling was done solely with the chemically dependent, absent of the significant people in their lives. Because of the lack of emphasis on relationships, I would watch these courageous individuals repeatedly fall short of their potential in relationships. I would often witness the return to using alcohol and other drugs when old feelings of low self-esteem, guilt, and shame resurfaced. Many would return to using to avoid the frustration and pain that occurred in close relationships. I began to realize, as did many of my colleagues, that working with an individual in such isolation was of little lasting use. The fact is, be it chemical dependency or any other addiction, the arena where addictions are played out is relationships. For this reason, any healing must include working on relationships with others.

Based on this belief I designed an intensive outpatient program that families attended together. They had the opportunity to spend time together in a group, focusing on relationship issues. Each night they would also have groups in which they would explore their own individual issues. When the program began we often encountered great resistance on the part of the family members. They were frequently firmly rooted in the belief that the problem was with the addict, and that if the addict cleaned up his or her act, things would get back to normal. Unfortunately, "normal" for these families was fleeting moments of love, along with much resentment, guilt, and fear. As a staff we felt so strongly about the importance of family involvement that we made it mandatory. If a spouse, parent, or important other was not willing to attend, we referred them elsewhere. To my amazement, less than 3 percent of the families refused to come. They often came kicking and screaming, but their coming showed that deep inside they knew that there had to be a better way for family members to relate to each other. After about a week of meeting daily, the changes were dramatic. Families saw that their secret feelings of being alone and unlovable were common among the other group members. Many group members had grown up with a hidden sadness and shame that they recognized, shared, and eventually worked through. The family members saw that they too were acting in compulsive and self-defeating ways; they awoke from the overwhelming feeling that it was up to them to control the addict's behavior. As I worked with these families it became clear to me that many of the issues that all people struggle with share a common theme: the fear of intimacy.

FAMILY ROLES AND THE FEAR OF LOVE

The fear of intimacy is really the fear of love, and it is epidemic in society today. We yearn for closeness yet live in a world where we feel that we must protect ourselves from others. We are busy building fences around our hearts. We grow up in families with parents who are less than perfect, and we often are surprised when we become "just like them." We long to remember our wholeness yet look for new things to get or new goals to achieve in order to feel better about ourselves. Or we turn to chemical substances, for with them, for a moment, we feel happy, powerful, and whole. Yet these methods boomerang, and our loneliness and despair only become compounded.

> *I found ways to forget my loneliness*
> *and in the process forgot who I was.*
>
> *Like clear water clouded*
> *by the turbulence of tides,*
> *fear became my guide while*
> *love seemed to be locked from my heart.*

I covered my fear with layers of armor,
and while I did I locked love out even more,
until I was afraid of love itself.

My shield became doing well and looking good.
Yet how strong could I make an eggshell?
I began to break,
and in the pieces I found who I was.

I grew up in a family that, from the outside, seemed perfect, yet I never felt quite right. My father was a successful psychiatrist, my mother a talented interior designer. My older brother and I were often referred to as good-looking young men. We had a beautiful home filled with most everything that a kid could want. All seemed flawless.

Though I felt that both my parents loved me, I also received many mixed messages. With my father, an alcoholic, I felt that I was either being spoiled with material items or being overworked or being punished. My mother was as devoted as any mother could possibly be, spending much time with my brother and me. Despite her good intentions I felt, on a deep level, my mother's pain in her marriage. By adopting different roles (rarely consciously) I felt that I was able to help the family not focus on my parents' unhappiness. I was not at all comfortable doing this, yet at that point I knew no other way. I felt distant, yet was also afraid of closeness. Not being able to say no or assert my feelings, I adopted ways of controlling levels of intimacy: I began to feign physical illnesses in an attempt to control where the spotlight went in my family.

One day, at thirteen, I went to my mother's office and complained of back pain. Through previous experience I knew that a physical complaint would capture the attention of my family. Today I don't remember if I was actually in physical pain, yet what followed set the stage for my adolescence. I was taken to the emergency room and given an injection of a powerful narcotic. Within minutes I felt the first relief from my hidden emotional pain that I had ever experienced. The drug gave me a false feeling of wholeness; I felt at ease with myself and my surroundings. I was admitted to the hospital and diagnosed as having a progressive disease characterized by a slow disintegration to the edges of the vertebrae due to physical growth. In an X-ray the vertebrae appeared as though they were being eaten away. Metaphorically, this was my psychological state: I felt that I was emotionally disintegrating while growing up.

I did not have the physical pain that apparently I was supposed to have. I began to fake the pain in order to get the all-important injections, for they were my relief, my island. From the hospital bed, with the euphoric narcotic high, I felt I was able to control much of my family's relations. I was the focus of attention. At thirteen my command station was my hospital bed, and my armor was my drugs. At the time much of this process of controlling others was unconscious. I was afraid and confused, and things just seemed to happen.

Within a few weeks I thickened my armor as the first of many body casts was plastered around me. This was when I first wondered if I was crazy. I felt like I had found safety, but I knew that this was not "normal." In order to feel what I thought was a little bit of love, I would time my narcotic injections to coincide with my family visits. Throughout my adolescence I had dozens of hospitalizations. At one point I had a hospital bed at home along with oral medication. I was afraid to leave my room, because it had everything I felt I needed to be safe: my bed, my drugs, my body cast, and my television. From my room, in a bizarre way, I felt that I had control over my family. As time went on my dependence on the drug increased and it would do less and less of a job of creating safety in euphoria. As I was less able to escape into the drug I became anxious, yet tried to keep it to myself. I feared being found out, yet felt very alone because nobody could see my true pain.

LOCKING LOVE OUT

Today, when I want to get a good picture of how afraid of intimacy I was, and how much I yearned for it, I remember an incident that occurred when I was fifteen. I had just received my largest body cast yet. The thick, cold plaster went from my pelvic area to over my head. I lay in a hospital bed in traction, weights hanging from my waist, neck, and jaw. I had been receiving an injection of a narcotic every four hours for a few weeks. My command post had become a fortress and my feelings lay deep beneath layers of plaster and drugs.

Because of the weights I could barely open my mouth to speak. My pain was trapped inside of me; love and intimacy could never make it through my thick armor. I did not doubt my family's love for me; I just could not let it in. I yearned for love, yet I thought if I let go of my role there would be no family there. This catch-22 would repeat itself in different forms for years to come.

One day, from my bed, I watched the news (my television was on eighteen hours a day). On the screen came a baby who lived in a bubble. There was a deficiency in the child's immune system. She could be handled only through thick plastic gloves, and faced a life of never feeling a human touch. I sobbed as I watched this story. Today, as I look back at many of my relationships, both as a child and as an adult, I feel that I know the pain of the heart of that child.

The hospitalizations decreased as I approached twenty, yet I continued to use drugs, which had come to include cocaine and alcohol in addition to the prescribed narcotic. I would have periods of not using drugs, but I would always use drugs when things got too close with someone, continuing my catch-22. Drugs allowed me to feel a false sense of closeness to people while at the same time keeping them away, staying in control of any situation.

It has been many years since I have used drugs. Looking back, I would not trade my life for another. Today I am able to feel the love of my parents, which was always there. The life that I have lived has taught me about addiction of all kinds, and I continue to find that it is possible to love and be loved in the moment, as I am. My experiences have taught me that there are two fundamental ways of being in the world: one is based on fear, the other on love. Today I choose love.

ON RESPONSIBILITY

As children we rarely consciously chose our roles. In our families of origin some of us became quiet and withdrawn, so much so that people barely knew we were there. Others of us became the high-achieving stars, giving our families a sense of pride. Some of us became the "sensitive" children, taking on our families' pain. It is important for us to see how we may still be playing out the roles we adopted as children, even though they may prevent us from experiencing love. As adults we can examine and change unwanted and outdated roles. The first step toward change is to realize,

> I choose the roles by which I live.
> I choose the feelings that I experience.

As human beings we are flexible, and have the ability to change our lives by shifting our perception of ourselves and the world. And as adults we have the ability to make choices, and so are responsible for our own lives.

Many of us slump our shoulders at the word *responsibility*. We often think of responsibility as being connected with something we have to do but don't really want to do. Usually the word *should* is associated with responsibility. Let me suggest to you that there is another way to look at responsibility. It is my belief that with true responsibility comes freedom. When we take responsibility for our lives we stop compulsively pointing our fingers at others and enter into a world where we make the decisions about our own lives. With choice and responsibility we have personal power.

> Responsibility is really the ability to respond.

THE FALLACY OF "I'M NOT OKAY THE WAY I AM"

Drugs were not the only way that I found to guard myself from love and my feelings of aloneness. I also found that I could create high goals for myself and hide in the pursuit of them. My high achievements were usually no different than the drugs: both served as safe hiding places from intimacy. And much of the time I was under double sedation: I chased a goal and did drugs to relieve the stress involved in my pursuit of the goal.

Like many adolescents in our society, I left high school confused about who I was. Within a few weeks of my arrival at the University of Oregon I was in a deep depression. I found that I could stave off the depression by getting lost in my work, so I began to immerse myself in my studies. Being overly studious appeared more acceptable than taking drugs, but for me they served the same purpose. I transferred later that year to Sonoma State University, which was near to my home in California. Somehow I believed that being there would help me to be happy. I found out that geographical moves are rarely the cure for depression. We take who we are wherever we go.

I continued to chase my goal of excelling at school, and found that I graduated the four-year B.A. program before two years had passed, with high honors. I had no idea who I was, but I was doing it well. A bizarre statement that described my life. On to graduate school at 19 years of age.

Our culture puts greater emphasis on what you do than it does on who you are. One of the first questions we ask people is "What do you do?" My family was no different than most, and at an early age I had seen that parents believed that the more you worked, the better. If you were suffering, this meant that you were doing well. At that time my father worked at least a twelve-hour day. I thought that this was what life was about and set out to do the same. I was under the illusion that if "what" I was doing was okay, then "who" I was should not need much attention. This error in thinking is fundamental to the addictive thought system.

ADDICTION AND THE CARROT SYNDROME

I built myself a machine, based on my parents' prototype: a rotating carrot machine. It sat firmly affixed to my head and held a carrot out at some distance. As long as I focused on the carrot in the distance I did not see myself in the here and now. As I pursued my juicy carrot my machine would bring it in closer and closer, and just as I was about to taste it, my machine would drop the carrot and produce a new one off in the distance. My machine had an audio component as well. I could hear people clapping as I successfully reeled in carrot after carrot, allowing me to feel some temporary satisfaction. As time went on the machine ran faster and faster, until one day I tired so much that I couldn't keep up the pace. I fell and lay on the ground alone, my machine broken beyond repair from the fall. There were no people to clap, just me in the here and now. I wept, because I knew at that moment I would never again be able to hide in my pursuit of goals. In my exhaustion I lay upon the earth, alone with my fears. I think that it was at that moment of despair that I truly started on the path of being a remembering human being, remembering love.

ATTACK, DEFENSE, AND ADDICTION

Our egos, in the addictive thought system, see us as vulnerable, guilty, and shameful, but always try to hide these feelings. Is it any surprise that building elaborate defense systems makes perfect sense to them? In a state of mind where fear is at the core, are not attack and defense a matter of protecting our safety? In a world based on separation, attack and defense are seen as normal and necessary tools for survival. If we are to find peace of mind, the core of this irrational thought system must be challenged.

The validity of attack and defense are upheld by the false belief that we are something other than love. When we perceive our self-esteem as being dependent on how much we have, we naturally become fearful that someone might take away what we have. When we draw arbitrary lines and divide the world up into good people and bad people, we find ways to prove that our divisions are valid. We play judge, passing verdicts hundreds of times a day. When we see ourselves as threatened in some way we launch our defense system. This scenario is based on an insane belief system that tells us we are not okay the way we are. The truth needs to be repeated often:

Love needs no defense.

In the addictive thought system our deceived minds tell us that defense is our key to safety. Now let us look at what defense actually is.

Over the years the world has drawn boundaries to signify where one country began and another ended. Each nation decided for itself whether another country was "good" or "bad." Of course, who is currently "bad" may at a later date be "good" and vice versa. In our own country we naturally always see ourselves as both good and right. Our borders are in place; we are now concerned that someone may threaten "our territory." Where fear is our guide, defenses seem totally reasonable.

As the world's defense systems became more advanced, this country developed nuclear weapons. In order to keep up the illusion that an elaborate defense brought safety, we gave the missiles catchy names, such as Peacekeeper. In all of this, there is one truth that our egos keep from us:

Our defenses bring what they were meant to guard against.

This is evident both on the international level and the individual level. On the international level we tell ourselves that we are increasing our defense because we are trying to avoid war. But what happens to the likelihood of war with each new weapon that is built? The likelihood of war increases because of the increased chance of accidental deployment and because of increased fear. As of this writing the superpowers are realizing this, to some small extent, and are attempting to reduce the number of weapons.

This same process occurs on an individual level. As we compulsively and addictively build our individual defenses, we increase the likelihood of conflict. It is an unfortunate vicious cycle that develops: we feel afraid, so we build defenses; as we build defenses, we become more afraid.

The pattern builds and develops into the cycle of attack and defense. In this cycle peace of mind is impossible, as is intimacy, and addiction is likely. An illustration of this cycle follows.

THE ALTERNATIVE TO ATTACK AND DEFENSE

Suppose that you could choose a different way of being in the world. Imagine that in your life you saw only two forms of communication. Either people were expressing love or they were calling for love. Think how differently you might relate to other people if you saw them, and yourself, through gentle and forgiving eyes. Such a love-centered view of the world is based on acceptance, opposed to attack, and forgiveness, as opposed to judgment. In contrast with the cycle of attack and defense, the following diagram illustrates the cycle of love-based thinking. The thought system that you choose at any given moment is up to you.

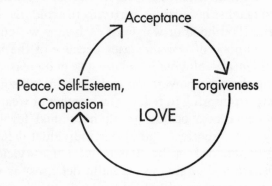

THE UNDERPINNINGS OF ATTACK AND DEFENSE

1. I become angry and attack when another person doesn't live up to my expectations.

The addictive thought system enters into relationships with the motto, Fulfill My Expectations and I Will Accept You, or the motto, I Will Be Happy If You——. When our peace of mind depends on another's behavior, sooner or later we will be disappointed. Our usual response to this disappointment is likely anger and blame. One may be somewhat passive with their anger and withdraw, saying, "I don't want to get hurt again." Some may be more aggressive, blaming and attacking the other person, saying, "I'm not happy and it's your fault." Either way, we are operating on the addictive principle that happiness comes from another person.

Love-based thinking says

I am responsible for my happiness.

2. When I become angry and attack another person, my hidden goal is to make the other person feel guilty.

In the addictive thought system we have the absurd belief that

a.   Somebody else is responsible for how I feel.

b. Making another feel guilty for what he or she has done will make me feel better.

Ask yourself right now: When has pointing a blaming finger ever given me any lasting happiness?

The truth about finger pointing is

> When I point a finger,
> I have three fingers pointing back at myself.

3. Attack and defense stem from my thinking that I am something other than love.

When I find myself verbally attacking another it is never because I am feeling good about myself. It is curious that what I really want, love and intimacy, is exactly what my defenses keep me from experiencing. The next time you find yourself caught up in the cycle of attack and defense, ask yourself, What am I defending against? Could I become aware of love by laying down my defenses?

Love-based thinking recognizes that

> I am love. There is nothing to defend.

4. Projection is the means I use to justify attack.

Many times in our relationships, we see unwanted and denied aspects of ourself manifesting themselves in other people. This is projection. The ego uses projection to make us feel justified in attacking others. As we choose to become aware of who we are, we also must confront the repressed parts of ourself. I refer to this as owning our projections. In so doing we clean the lens through which we see others.

Love-Based thinking recognizes that

> Attack is never justified.

5. Attack is really a defense, and defenses always bring what they were meant to guard against.

It is necessary to realize the following before you can experience consistent peace of mind and unconditional love:

a. Every time we attack another person, we injure ourself.
b. Whenever we are defensive, we are turning our back on love.
c. If we want love, it is our attack thoughts that are in need of healing.
d. It is our defensiveness that keeps us feeling separate and alone.
e. As long as we are in the cycle of attacking and defending, we are stuck in an addictive cycle.

The comical truth is that

Punching your reflection in the mirror hurts your hand.

6. Attack and defense never bring me what I really want.

If what you want is peace of mind, you must realize that attack and defense only result in conflict. We must question the logic of the ego, which states that we are in constant need of defense. The truth is that your safety lies in our defenselessness.

Defensiveness brings fear.

Defenselessness brings love.

7. Attack and defense preserve guilt and escalate fear.

Guilt and fear keep the wheels of the addictive thought system turning. The ego tells us that fear is real and that we are in constant danger. We play the game of hot potato, where we quickly toss our guilt to the next person, thinking that we are getting rid of it.
    If I want to be happy, I must see that

Tossing my guilt to another person
does not get rid of it.

8. Attack and defense are a call for love.

There is no one who does not want to be loved. The problem is that because of the ego's addictive thought system a person can become confused and end up protecting himself or herself from love while keeping fear alive and well. As hard as it is to see, when someone behaves defensively or attacks you, he or she is crying for help. If you can respond in love the cycle will eventually cease.

The core of the love-based thought system is the following:

Where there is fear, love is the answer.

9. Forgiveness is the key to happiness.

Happiness—peace of mind—begins with a change in how we perceive the world and ourself. Forgiveness is the gentle letting go of the past. It allows us to view the world and ourself through the clarity of the present moment. We are constantly choosing between forgiveness and the cycle of attack and defense.

Forgiveness is my single function
where peace of mind is my single goal.

TRUST VERSUS trust

In my practice I see many people in relationships with chemically dependent people. These individuals share many common feelings, thoughts, and behaviors. The constellation of these is referred to as codependency, although many codependent people do not have relationships with chemically dependent people. Working with codependency has made me more aware of an issue with which many people have problems: trust.

Mary came to see me after completing the family component of a treatment program where her husband, Jeff, was for cocaine addiction. Early in our first session Mary became teary, and, with frustration in her voice, said, "I just don't know if I can ever trust him again. It seems that as soon as I begin to count on someone I am slowly crushed. I find myself either trying to please that person or withdrawing from that person." The intensity of Mary's frustration and pain suggested that this problem had not begun with this relationship. We began to explore her relationship and family history.

Over the next several sessions Mary described growing up in a home where her mother was an alcoholic. She said that she felt that her mother loved her, yet her mother's behavior was wildly erratic: sometimes she was sober, loving, and attentive; at other times she was drunk, emotionally unavailable, and explosive. Mary learned that she couldn't trust her mother, as much as she wished that she could.

Mary often turned to her father for comfort. In her early years he was there for her. As the years went on, her father became involved in his work in order to stay away from home. She found that there was really nobody she could trust. Mary secretly thought that maybe the family problems were her fault; she still carried this guilt when I met her.

When Mary met Jeff she thought that she had finally found someone whom she could trust. After six years of marriage Jeff began using cocaine. Within ten months Mary's world had shattered.

Over several months of our working together, Mary worked through much of her pain regarding the mixed messages her parents had given her. She became able, for the first time, to feel angry at her parents while recognizing that she was not to blame for the family's problems. Eventually she worked through the anger and forgave them. Mary had a more difficult time with Jeff, because on a day-to-day basis she was afraid to trust him. This fear kept her from any true intimacy with her husband.

Mary learned that there are actually two types of trust: Trust, with a capital T and trust, with a lowercase t. Trust, with a capital T, is based on love. Mary became aware that she could see the light of love in Jeff without being attached to his behavior. This helped Mary let go of her need to control Jeff. Mary recognized that Jeff's behavior was about Jeff, not about her. She saw that she was not responsible for his behavior. She chose to stop seeing his behavior as a barometer of her self-esteem.

Mary saw that trust, with a lowercase t, was based on consistency of behavior. Jeff would need to be in recovery for a while before Mary would trust him. She found, however, that she could love Jeff, while still holding him accountable for his actions. In short, she didn't have to shut off her heart from love because of fear of Jeff's behavior.

In your daily life, if you find you are shutting yourself off from love, remember the following:

1. I can always see the light of love in other people, regardless of their behavior. I can Trust in love.
2. Other people's behavior is about them, not about me. Let me take responsibility for my feelings and actions and allow others to do the same.
3. I cannot control or predict other people's actions. I can choose between building a fence around my heart and identifying with love.

CHAPTER SEVEN

Learning To Love Ourselves

When we are caught in addiction it is impossible to experience love. Compulsivity and peace of mind are mutually exclusive. It is my belief that much addictive behavior stems from trying to cover up or run away from deep feelings of aloneness. Rather than feel our aloneness we become focused on controlling, getting, judging, defending, and attacking, as ways of looking away from our loneliness. Our addictions slowly become the walls behind which we hide. Eventually our walls become so high that instead of simply hiding we become prisoners of our own making. The guards in the prison of addiction are our egos, while the bars of our cells are forged with our irrational beliefs. We sit upon cold gray cement in our dark and isolated cells, thinking that there is no escape.

In order to become free of our addictions we must first identify the irrational beliefs that keep us stuck where we are.

IRRATIONAL BELIEFS OF THE ADDICTED MIND

1. My self-esteem is dependent upon my being approved of by everybody on this planet.

Unanimous approval is highly unlikely, and this belief results in another one of the ego's vicious cycles:

a. I try to please other people so I will feel good about myself.
b. I eventually fail because I can't always please everybody. Failure brings on feelings of guilt, which lead to feelings of low self-worth.
c. To compensate for feelings of low self-worth, I become even more of a people pleaser.

In love-based thinking I realize that

My self-esteem is not dependent upon pleasing others.
Approval seeking takes me away from who I am.

2. If I am to consider myself worthwhile, I must excel, achieve, win, and display glowing competence at all times, in all places, and at all costs.

How brittle self-esteem can become. Is it any surprise that such a belief leads to addiction? This belief is based on a fear that if you let down your guard for even a second you might slip and be found out to be incompetent. The fear of being found out as a fake is prevalent in our society. Some years ago a study revealed that a large number of individuals in high-level, respected positions felt, deep down that, they were not qualified. These individuals felt that one day they might be discovered as frauds. The result of this belief is that the individual runs on a treadmill, oftentimes with high achievements, yet his or her inner experience is one of feeling deeply inadequate, not enough.

Love-based thinking reflects the truth about who you are:

My self-worth is not based solely upon what I do or achieve.
I am enough right now.

3. All things that go wrong in my life are caused by other people. These people need to be blamed and punished.

To avoid our own underlying feelings of inadequacy we may blame other people. Sometimes we may feel so out of control in our life that we irrationally think that blaming and punishing another person will somehow give us back a little bit of control. Fear is at the core of this belief. While we run from fear we cannot ever look at the source of the real problem: our addictive mind.

Love-based thinking recognizes that

Healing must begin in my own mind.

4. If external situations in my life are not exactly how I want them to be, I must feel tense, worry endlessly, and expect a disaster to occur within seconds.

The ego has a surefire way to keep us from looking at ourself and our belief system. The ego encourages us to become totally preoccupied with the chaos around us. It may be a new thought for you that the situation is *not* the determiner of your experience. You may have become used to feeling happy when things are going your way, and unhappy when you don't like the situation. We can behave like a robot programmed with responses to all situations. We can become so caught up in trying to make the outside world to our liking that we forget about our inner life. When we compulsively try to control external circumstances, we guarantee ourself a life void of lasting peace.

The one thing about trying to control situations is that the job is never quite done. You will be able to find something else that needs to be controlled. Conversely, as you become more comfortable with who you are, the need to control things will diminish.

In 1982 I spent time with Mother Teresa at her Missions of Charity in India. Through her I saw firsthand that it is possible to experience peace of mind even when surrounded by hunger and death. I believe that she saw these abandoned children and dying people as being in need of love and respect. Her focus was on providing them with this, while asking for nothing in return. Being with her was probably the first time that I truly believed that peace of mind is a choice, that every person is capable of unconditional love, and that happiness is not dependent upon the external situation.

I am not suggesting that we should not care about what is happening in the world. I am stating that where we must begin is where we must also end, and that is with examining our own mind. In order to live a peaceful life you must recognize that we have control over our own feelings and reactions.

Love-based thinking states

> If I want to change my life, I must first change my mind.
> What I experience is based upon my thoughts and beliefs.

5. If something negative happened in the past, I should be very concerned about it repeating itself in the future. It will help if I keep dwelling on the possibility of it occurring.

There is nothing written in stone that states that the past will repeat itself, yet many people run their lives on this premise. This belief leads to a lack of trust, a guardedness. The irony is that simply dwelling on a possible negative outcome can cause it to occur. If we put enough energy into thinking something will happen, good or bad, it just might. And when we see our negative prediction come true we increase our commitment to worrying about the next catastrophe. This, in turn, creates another one of the ego's vicious cycles.

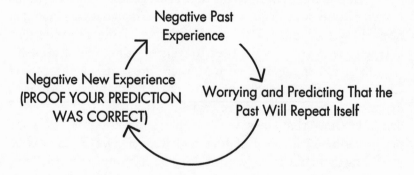

I lived in Mexico for a year and saw the effects of this belief demonstrated in an ironic way. Montezuma's revenge is a problem with travel south of the border. It was my observation that people visiting Mexico approached this fact in one of three ways:

1. They ignore it, eating and drinking everyting in sight.
2. They realized that they were not immune to bacteria. They enjoyed their food, ate lightly at first, and avoided obviously unsanitary situations. Beyond that, they did not preoccupy themselves with the situation.
3. They worried constantly about it, questioning everyone about the food until the proprietor wanted to throw it at them. They constantly thought about how awful they felt the last time that they had had diarrhea.

What I observed in my casual study was that members of group 1 and group 3 became ill with more or less the same frequency. Those in group 2 were the least likely to be counting the tiles in the bathroom. The point of the story is that excessive worry does more harm than good. Because of the power of thought we attract that upon which we dwell. This power can be used to bring either positive or negative experiences into our life. The choice is ours.

In letting go of worry we begin to experience joy. When we are preoccupied with the future and worrying about the past we are likely miserable. As human beings we have a powerful brain, yet we may have problems with three simple facts about time:

The past is past.
The future is in the future.
The present is present.

6. If I avoid painful issues and stuff down my emotions, I will be safe and happy.

Despite popular opinion, repression and procrastination are *not* the keys to happiness. Through our addictions we have attempted to push down our feelings of anger, unworthiness, and shame. When we stop our addictive behavior by confronting the addictive thought system, repressed pain will surface. It is by allowing this process to unfold (usually with the help of a friend, a therapist, or a sponsor in a twelve-step program) and working through our pain that we once again become feeling human-beings. Procrastination is an indirect way of saying, "I don't trust myself, my intuition, or God." Our pain makes us afraid to move in any direction; we become stuck. We procrastinate about changing the situation. The more afraid we become, the more we procrastinate. As we procrastinate we adopt addictive ways of being in order to further avoid our feelings and create more reasons to not like ourself.

In contrast with repression and procrastination, love-based thinking states

> I trust in the unfolding of my life.
> Love has never abandoned me.
> I need but open my heart to it.

7. I am weak and need to be dependent on somebody or something else.

You may have a feeling of being weak, incomplete, or somehow insufficient. Even being alone for a few hours may make you uncomfortable. You may find that drugs or other addictions give you temporary relief, yet deep down the feeling of incompleteness persists.

When I was a kid, my family enjoyed doing jigsaw puzzles. Sometimes we could not find a piece. After we would search for a certain piece for hours we would joke about the puzzle being sent from the manufacturer with a piece missing. Each time this happened I became convinced that someone at the factory had a cruel sense of humor and had withheld one or two pieces. Eventually the missing piece would always eventually turn up.

None of us came into this world with a piece missing. It may take patience and perseverance to remember our wholeness, but it is there.

This is not to say that we don't need intimacy with other people. But being in a dependent position is not intimacy, it is dependence, and is based on a belief that we lack something in ourself. When we become aware of our wholeness we can then begin to truly share ourself with others. We can also allow ourself to be nurtured.

Share who you are with another.
Don't look to another to make up for a lack in yourself.

8. I should be very involved in, and upset about, other people's problems.

When people learn that I am a psychologist their first response is often, "Don't you get depressed listening to problems all day?" I suggest to them that it is possible to be of service to others without taking on their problems and their pain. Each of us can be compassionate without taking on suffering. You may think that being helpful means being overly identified with another person's pain. Though it is important to acknowledge the person's pain, it is equally important to see that person's health as well. If I see the underlying health and wholeness in a person, I feel whole. If I identify only with the pain, I feel only pain.

Many of us may jump into solving other people's problems as a way of giving yourself some sort of self-esteem. This is just another form of addiction: we think that doing something or problem-solving will bring us happiness. When we stop being a super problem solver, we will probably feel a shame and a low self-esteem that the addiction has covered up It is through sharing this pain with another human being that we can move toward healing ourself. From this healed, whole place, we can truly be of service. Recognize that

Fixing you will not fix me.

9. There is one right way to view the world.

If you grew up in an alcoholic or dysfunctional family, you may think this way. To compensate for the craziness and inconsistency that you witnessed, you may defend yourself by seeing the world as divided into good and bad, right and wrong. This belief locks out intimacy. The subtext of this belief is, My safety lies in believing that everything is black and white, that there are no gray areas in life. Recognizing that this rigid view of the world lacks truth brings underlying anxiety to the surface. This is because when you give up rigidity you must confront life's ambiguities.

We can become addicted to a certain way of viewing ourself and the world, despite the fact that such a view keeps us from experiencing closeness with another. When you find yourself lacking the closeness to another that you want, remember:

> There is another way to look at this.
> The world is not always clearly black and white.
> If I am attached to being right,
> I am shutting the door on learning the lessons of love.

10. I am limited in what I can do and the happiness that I can experience.

There is an entire vocabulary devoted to the belief that people are limited. I refer to these words as love blockers, because they inhibit our ability to experience love and creativity by reinforcing the addictive thought system. Love blockers are words that can be seen as the mortar that holds the bricks of the addictive thought system together. If we remove the mortar (love blockers), the bricks (addictive beliefs) are more easily removed. Some examples of love blockers follow.

I *doubt* if I could succeed. I know that I *should* do it, *but* it is too *difficult*. Besides, nobody else seems to be able to succeed; it is *impossible*. And I've *tried* it before; I *can't* do it. *If only* things were different. I ought to do it, but I have this *limitation* that prevents me.

In addition to the italicized love blockers already mentioned, many other words become love blockers when used for categorizing, evaluating, or judging yourself or others.

Most people use at least a few love blockers, and everyone has his or her personal favorites. Yet with conscious effort we can eliminate these words from our vocabulary. In doing so we will make giant strides toward uprooting the addictive belief system.

Richard Bach, in his book *Illusions*, says one sentence that summarizes love blockers: "Argue for your limitations and sure enough, they're yours."

The following two pages show, side by side, a slightly abbreviated form of the irrational beliefs of the addictive thought system and the peaceful alternative of the love-based thought system. You may find it helpful to refer to these lists in times of conflict to see your choices.

IRRATIONAL BELIEFS OF THE EGO

1. My self-esteem is dependent upon my being approved of by everybody.
2. If I am to consider myself worthwhile, I must always achieve, win, succeed.
3. Other people are to blame for things that go wrong in my life.
4. I should always worry if things are not exactly how I think that they should be.
5. I should always dwell on the possibility of the past repeating itself.
6. Stuffing down my feelings makes my life safe and happy.
7. I am weak and need to be dependent on someone or something.
8. I should become upset about, and preoccupy myself with, others' problems.
9. My way of seeing the world is the right way.
10. I am limited in what I can do.

CODEPENDENCY AS ADDICTION

The word *codependency* refers to a constellation of emotions, beliefs, and behaviors based on the individual's feelings of shame, low self-worth, and fear of intimacy. There are currently many excellent books on codependency.

If you believe that your happiness is in some way dependent upon the outside world, you will try to control others and your environment. In the end, control becomes a slippery friend. Ironically, once you are addicted to someone or something, you spend much time trying to control the addiction itself. Addiction and the need to control are tandem partners in making peace of mind impossible.

> When you are trying to control another person,
> intimacy is impossible.

Most addicted people (including codependents) with whom I have worked come to see me in a tired state, as if they were on the last mile of a marathon. Sometimes a person doesn't appear tired, but later will laugh at how much effort it took him or her to look as though everything were fine. Later, when questioned as to what was so exhausting, the person will speak of the endless effort it took to try to control other people and their environment.

Anne came to see me after attending a workshop on codependency. She had identified with much of the material presented and wanted to take a more in-depth look at her life. Anne was forty-two, had grown up in a workaholic home, and was married to a recovering alcoholic. Anne was what most people would call a responsible woman. She held down a professional job and was raising two children. She spent a great deal of her time taking care of other people and practically no time taking care of herself. In our work together Anne found that her self-esteem was tied to trying to solve other people's problems, being approved of by others, and relieving others' pain. Anne had always put other people's needs and feelings first, at the expense of her own. As a result of all this, Anne found herself void of happiness and living a

SANE BELIEFS OF LOVE-BASED THINKING

1. My self-esteem is not based upon pleasing others.
2. I am complete, full of love, and worthwhile this very inst
3. Healing my life begins in my own mind.
4. If I desire change I must first look to my mind.
5. The past is past. The future is in the future. The prese present.
6. Opening my heart to love makes my life full and happy
7. Through sharing who I am with others, I come to know I am. I lack nothing to begin this today.
8. Fixing you will not fix me.
9. Love and forgiveness will show me the way to serenity.
10. I am limitless.

life where guilt and shame were the primary feelings, and control and manipulation were the primary behaviors.

At an early age Anne had assumed responsibility for other people's feelings. As a child, when one of her parents was angry about anything, she would feel responsible. As an adult, when her husband did something that went against her values, she would feel the shame and embarrassment that he seemed not to feel. Regardless of how strong her feelings were, she would rarely express them, because she feared the other person's reaction. As Anne became more and more caught in this cycle of codependency, she became less and less aware of what she actually was feeling. At the time Anne entered therapy with me she was not sure what she was feeling, and had difficulty identifying or expressing any opinions of her own.

Much of Anne's difficulty came from her belief, deep down, that she didn't have a right to her feelings. She would consistently put others first, at the expense of her own growth. When it came to her family, it was as though she had feeling radar, and always knew how everybody else felt. The problem was that she rarely could identify how she was feeling. As our work progressed, Anne began to be aware of her feelings. Fear of rejection, loneliness, and shame came into her awareness for the first time in many years. These feelings had lain beneath the surface, and had fueled her codependency.

After seeing Anne and many other codependents, I have come to realize that codependency is an addiction in and of itself. Following is a list of ten beliefs that I consider to be the bedrock of codependency. After each belief is the feeling or characteristic that results from it. The overall result of these beliefs is that the individual develops an obsessive need to control people, places, and things, in order to cover feelings of inadequacy, shame, and fear. In the attempt to control, the person loses the awareness of the presence of love.

CORE BELIEFS OF CODEPENDENCY

1. **Belief:** I am responsible for other people's feelings and behaviors. What other people do is a reflection of who I am.

Result: I feel guilty much of the time. I feel good about myself only when everybody else is doing okay.

2. **Belief:** Other people's feelings are more important than my own.

   Result: I have a hard time identifying my feelings, and often question what I feel.

3. **Belief:** I have to be needed by others in order to be loved and feel worthwhile.

   Result: I choose relationships where I nurture others, but rarely receive nurturing myself. I put other people's needs and desires first. I feel guilty if I take any time just for me. I have being needed confused with being loved. I can be there for everybody except for myself.

4. **Belief:** Other people's opinions and values are more important than my own.

   Result: I am not aware of having many opinions, and any that I do have I am afraid to voice. I have a difficult time making decisions. I am spongelike, absorbing what others feel, think, and value.

5. **Belief:** I don't have the right to feel as I do.

   Result: I am fearful of other people's responses to my feelings. I compulsively worry about what other people think of me. I feel small and powerless, and often feel resentful. I push away my values and feelings in order to feel accepted by others.

6. **Belief:** My relationships with others is a statement of who I am. Likewise, their behavior is a public statement of who I am.

   Result: I am afraid of being rejected. It is hard for me to become close to other people. If my relationships are good, I feel good; if trouble arises, my life falls apart. I am always loyal, even if my loyalty to others is harmful to me.

7. **Belief:** I am shameful.

   Result: I minimize my feelings and try to please others in order to avoid my feelings of low self-worth. I can't let others really know me, because they wouldn't like what they saw. I don't feel worthy of love.

8. **Belief:** I need to dictate other people's behavior to be happy.

Result: My peace of mind is determined by how others are behaving. I have difficulty acknowledging good qualities in myself. I am always the peacekeeper, smoothing over any conflict.

9. **Belief:** I am inadequate.

   Result: I think that I always must justify my feelings. No matter what I do, I don't feel good enough. I'm always taking on tasks and projects in order to feel some sense of self-esteem. I am prone to workaholism. I'm afraid that if I let my guard down, someone will find out how incompetent I am.

10. **Belief:** I need to be perfect all of the time.

    Result: I judge everything that I do, say, or think with harshness. I am never satisfied or approving of myself. I am full of self-condemnation and empty of self-love.

It is important to realize the results of your thinking so that you may look to new ways of being in the world. But such a realization, in and of itself, does not necessarily lead to change. This book can open your eyes to ways in which you keep love away. Whether you begin to open your heart to the power of love is up to you. The following are ways in which you can, right now, begin to open up your heart to love:

1. Choose to have the willingness, the openness, and the desire to feel your feelings, instead of hiding in addiction.
2. Practice, each hour, letting go of the past and letting go of controlling other people, places, and things.
3. *Consciously* affirm who you are (love, wholeness, and light) instead of *unconsciously* affirming who you actually are not (unworthy and needy).

LETTING GO: GIVING FORGIVENESS A PLACE TO HAPPEN

There are days when I feel as though I am a juggler trying to keep twelve balls in the air at once—while hopping on one foot. Everything seems to be demanding my attention; it seems like I can't complete anything. At these times it is especially important that I let go.

I often use the following imagery to help me let go. I invite you to read the next paragraph, and then shut your eyes and spend about five minutes repeating the process for yourself.

Letting Go: A Visualization

Picture yourself sitting by a gentle stream, the water flowing gently past you. You are seated on soft grass, feeling the warm sun upon your face. The sound of the stream, the rush of the clear water over smooth rocks, begins to relax you. Imagine that the water runs through you, cleansing your body and mind of any unwanted tension. After you have been sitting by the stream for a while, you notice that a seemingly endless parade of golden leaves float, one at a time, past you and out of sight. On each leaf place a worry, a negative belief about yourself, or a judgmental thought. Feel the sense of inner calm as you release your first thought. Now place another thought on another leaf. Again, feel your body relax as the leaf floats away. With each leaf, one by one, watch the unwanted contents of your mind float down the stream and out of sight. As you do so, your mind begins to become cleansed and calm. As your mind clears, you begin to feel lighter. Your shoulders relax, your breathing becomes full. Your heart becomes open and more full of love. As you let go of your worries, negativity, and judgments, you begin to look at yourself and the world with loving eyes.

This exercise can be likened to taking out the garbage. You may go through life accumulating worries, negative beliefs about yourself, judgments, and miscellaneous other "garbage thoughts." And when you are ready to go to sleep at night, you take your trash can and empty the contents into your bed, and then climb in between the garbage-strewn sheets. Upon waking you diligently put the garbage back in the can and set out on yet another day of garbage collecting. The problem is that you spend a lot of time putting garbage in the can and no time emptying the can. Take care of your true home—your heart and mind—by beginning to let go of your garbage thoughts. When you adopt a daily practice of letting go, you will naturally begin to feel love in your life.

In Letting Go . . .

In letting go we allow love to naturally unfold, instead of trying to bring about a certain outcome.

In letting go we do not stop to care for other people. Instead we see that we do not need to do it for other people.

In letting go we realize that we can't control other people's behavior, but we can change how we perceive others and ourselves.

In letting go we become love focused instead of fear focused, thus completely changing our views of ourselves and the world.

In letting go we stop blaming others and we release guilt. We allow ourselves and others to feel and express feelings.

In letting go of control we extend unconditional love, absent of an attachment to the outcome.

In letting go of judgment we allow ourselves and others to be human beings. We realize that a judging mind is not a peaceful mind.

In letting go we see that holding onto the past is the last thing we want to do.

In letting go we stop denying love the opportunity to express itself.

In short, in letting go we forgive ourselves and others.

AFFIRMING WHO YOU ARE

We spend a great deal of time unconsciously reinforcing the addictive thought system. We engage in endless negative self-talk and rarely hold anything positive and true in our mind for more than a few seconds. When we look in the mirror we may have an easier time seeing a person we are critical of than seeing the light of love shining back at us.

In the cycle of addiction our beliefs about who we are become distorted. It is up to us to start giving the cultivation of love as much time as we have given to fanning the fire of fear. Following is a list of affirming statements that help to reverse negative self-talk. I suggest that you choose one affirmation each day and repeat it to yourself for one minute every waking hour. That is a mere one-sixtieth of your waking day devoted to the cultivation of love. It is not much time, but you will find that all love needs is a small opening to begin to fill your heart. Love is like light. When you enter a dark room and turn on the light, the darkness immediately disappears; the light is everywhere. So it is with love.

The affirmations that follow are specifically designed for those who see codependent traits in themselves. They are also universal concepts in that they can benefit everyone.

TRUTHS ABOUT MYSELF

1. I am surrounded by love. I am safe. There is nothing to fear.
2. I am worthwhile and lovable just as I am this moment. I need do nothing today to prove myself worthy.
3. My feelings need no justification. Today I can feel and express my feelings.
4. I am gentle with myself. Self-criticism only injures me.
5. I am not alone. I am one with the universe.
6. The past is over. I am forgiven.
7. I choose my feelings. I am not controlled by people, places, or things.
8. I am important. Because of this I can take time for myself today without feeling guilty.
9. Love is always available to me. When I find myself in conflict I need but change my mind.
10. I deserve love. I am whole and good.

CHAPTER EIGHT

Growing as a Couple: Moving from Fear to Love

In working with couples I often find that they have lost sight of who they are, both as individuals and as a couple. Most often they come to me knowing intuitively that they love each other, but they have become confused and lost in endless fear, guilt, defense, and attack.

When we operate in the addictive thought system, we are like a rat in a maze. Each path promises a positive outcome, but each path that is taken only leads deeper into despair. A couple who wants to know love in all its depth must be willing to go beyond the addictive thought system to the new, yet ancient, territory of love.

Alan and Jackie had been married for five years and had two children, ages two and four, when they came to me. They said that they were thinking about divorce. They stated that they could not say a word to each other without starting an argument. Minutes into our first session they were at each other's throats with accusations. Already sensing that I knew the answer, I asked them why, if they were so miserable with each other, they wanted to stay together. There was a quiet moment. I saw tears well up for both of them. Then each said that it was because they loved each other. In their voices it was clear that they did. They did not want help solely for the children's sake or only because they were afraid to be alone.

These things were certainly a consideration, but they really wanted help because deep down they loved each other, but didn't know how to truly feel and express it. Fear was choking out the roots of their love.

As our work together progressed, it was revealed that both of them came from difficult and painful childhoods. Alan had been left, much of the time, with babysitters or by himself. Both his parents were distant and very career oriented, absent from the home much of the time. The only time Alan had seen any affection from his parents was when he did something that made them proud. Most of the time Alan had been told that he could do better or that he was wrong. As an adult Alan became an overachiever who never felt that what he did was sufficient.

Jackie had grown up in a family that always just squeaked by financially. Her father started out his work life as a laborer. He later opened his own business, but he never did very well. Jackie had two brothers, both of whom were in and out of jail. Her mother and father always looked to Jackie to be the one in the family to do well, often saying "You're our only hope." Yet when Jackie did do well, her parents expressed jealousy and resentment. With the mixed message of "Do well but don't do too well," Jackie ended up always feeling either incompetent or guilty. It didn't matter if things were going "well" or "poorly," Jackie could not feel good about herself.

Alan never felt that he could fully trust someone who was expressing praise, because he felt that close on the heels of praise would be criticism. He believed that he had to hide most of his emotions if he wanted any love. And his feeling that no matter what he did, it was not sufficient, was reinforced by Jackie; she was afraid to appear unsure of herself, so she acted in an opinionated fashion. In relating to one another, Alan and Jackie were playing out their patterns of the past, unable to see each other through the eyes of love. When Jackie would say something as minor as "Did you go to the store today?" Alan would feel unaccepted and criticized. He felt as he had as a child, wanting love but never feeling like he could do enough. Unable to state these feelings of wanting love and acceptance, he instead would have fits of rage that even he could not understand. His rage was boiling up from repressed feelings of inadequacy and thinking that he constantly needed to defend himself from criticism.

One way Jackie could feel like she was in control was to be a compulsive fault finder. She was afraid to look less than perfect herself, so she projected her own feelings of inadequacy onto Alan. And, at the same time, deep down she felt guilty for any competence that she did have.

In short, Alan became angry at the drop of a hat as a way of avoiding his feelings of being not enough. And Jackie criticized constantly as a way of avoiding her own feelings of being not enough. Consequently, neither one ever felt accepted or loved simply for who he or she was.

In our work together each of them became able to see his or her own pattern. Alan and Jackie began to talk to each other more about their individual fears, and what it was like for them to grow up feeling so isolated. As they began to see this commonality, their love for each other began to shine through their fears. Instead of raging, Alan was able to tell Jackie how alone he felt, and how he needed to feel accepted instead of criticized. When Jackie was tempted to find fault with Alan, she would instead tell him how hard it was for her not to always be in control. She began to share with him how she felt distant from people when she played the part of being perfect.

Though the story of Alan and Jackie is, of course, unique, the solution to their problems can be used by any couple who want to experience love more consistently in their relationship. A brief outline of this solution follows:

1. Know that the cycles of the addictive thought system are learned patterns of thinking and behaving, and therefore can also be unlearned.

2. Recognize that a more loving and peaceful existence is possible.

3. Understand that the purpose of the relationship is to learn the lessons of love, not to reinforce the past.

4. Make a conscious effort to talk directly about your fears and hidden thoughts. As your partner begins

to know who you are, *you* will begin to know who you are. Healing does not occur in a vacuum.

5. Know and practice the three magical words that lay the groundwork for love to emerge. The phrase *Choose once again* can redirect your mind even if you are already caught in a negative cycle. No matter how off center you may be, you have the power to redirect yourself. For example, if you are in an angry cycle, you can learn to catch yourself and mentally say, "Choose once again." This allows you to begin to speak from your inner feelings, thus creating closeness instead of separation.

6. Decide as a couple that you will not spend your time trying to make each other feel guilty, which always results in conflict. Resolve that you two are partners in guilt busting. Pledge together to practice forgiveness. Become messengers of love, instead of messengers of guilt.

The addictive thought system manifests itself in relationships through many irrational thoughts. On the next page is a list of what I feel to be the five most common addictive thoughts that keep couples from growing in love. Following this list is another that shows five parallel love-based thoughts that allow couples to enhance their relationships. These lists are not meant to be complete, so you may want to add to them any irrational and rational thoughts that come to mind.

THOUGHTS THAT ENCOURAGE
COUPLES TO STAY STUCK

1. If I have to work on the relationship, something must be wrong. Two people who love each other don't have to work on their relationship.
2. When we have an argument, somebody has to be wrong. I should try my best to prove that something is your fault. I should also keep score, making sure that I am right most of the time.
3. It is better not to talk about negative feelings. If I pretend that everything is okay, everything will be. If I don't talk, I won't have to feel.
4. If I make my partner feel guilty, it will make me feel better. Blaming is always a good defense.
5. Whenever I give to you I should be able to expect something from you in return.

THOUGHTS THAT ENCOURAGE
COUPLES TO OPEN TO LOVE

1. In our relationship it is my goal to not hide who I am from you. At times this is not easy, and in these times I will ask for your help.
2. Knowing who I am involves honoring all of who you are. If together we look beyond fault, there is no dark cloud that our love together cannot banish.
3. Love cannot be found alone. When I withhold feelings I turn my back on the opportunity to learn of love and deepen my relationship with you and with myself.
4. My goal, which I share with my partner, is to overcome guilt, not reinforce it. My partner and I do this through forgiveness.
5. Every loving thought reinforces itself. Giving and receiving are, in truth, one.

I think that our relationships are the classrooms where we have the greatest opportunity to learn how to live out the love-based thought system. I have certainly found this to be true in my relationship with my wife. In our marriage celebration Carny and I, along with our friend the Reverend George McLaird, who performed the ceremony, tried to put into words what we believed about a committed relationship. Here is an excerpt from our vows:

> Marriage is at its best when
> we love and marry our best friend.
> At its highest,
> marriage is motivated by unconditional love,
> where we seek the truth in each event,
> and act on that truth.
> As we grow in understanding and acceptance
> of ourself and our partner,
> we open our heart and welcome love.

If I focus on understanding and acceptance, how can I help but experience love?

Daily Lessons

INTRODUCTION TO DAILY LESSONS

Part One provides a framework and some exercises for better understanding the cycles of addiction and how peace of mind is always a possible alternative. This section, Part Two, offers more exercises, presented here as daily lessons. It is by actually practicing the exercises that the addictive thought system can be dismantled and peace of mind can be more consistently experienced. Do not worry about believing all of the ideas; simply be open to the power of love. The exercises presented offer you a systematic and practical means for living a life free of addiction. Each of the twenty-one daily lessons is intended to help you remove blocks to the awareness of love.

HOW TO PROCEED WITH THE DAILY LESSONS

The daily lessons and the discussions that accompany them are brief, practical, and direct. The emphasis is not on theory, but rather on experience. To receive the most benefit from the daily lessons, proceed with them in the manner outlined in the following paragraphs.

Each morning, soon after arising, review the lesson (and its accompanying discussion) for the day. Start with Lesson One and sequentially practice one lesson per day. Practice in a quiet place, one where you won't be disturbed. Relax and spend about five minutes reading the lesson and the discussion slowly, keeping the lesson (which appears in boldface) and the discussion in the forefront of your thoughts. During your practice time concentrate on the lesson and the discussion, and let any distracting thoughts go. If an unwanted thought interrupts your concentration, simply acknowledge its presence and then gently let it go.

During the day, when stressful situations crop up, slowly and thoughtfully repeat the lesson to yourself. This is especially useful in times of conflict. Apply the lesson to *all* people and *all* situations that you encounter. Do not make exceptions. Review the lesson periodically during the day for a few moments, preferably hourly. You may find it helpful either to carry the book with you or to copy the lesson onto a three-by-five card. In the evening, preferably right before retiring, take five minutes or more to review the lesson and the discussion again. Think about your day and how the lesson applies to specific circumstances that were difficult for you. When you have completed all twenty-one lessons in this manner, begin again and repeat the series. This continuous practice is best maintained until you find yourself applying the lessons spontaneously and consistently in your life.

In brief, your daily practice consists of four parts: a morning practice session, application of the lesson to stressful situations that occur throughout the day, an hourly review, and an evening review.

LESSON ONE

I have given everything I see in this room (on this street, from this window, in this place) all the meaning it has for me.

Because this lesson completely contradicts the addictive thought system, it can be confusing at first. This lesson says that there is nothing inherent in anything that gives it a set value or meaning. You alone define what is important to you and what is not.

When you are addicted to something or someone, it is because you have invested too much in one area, thinking it would bring happiness. You compulsively pursue something that continually leaves you feeling empty inside. A true statement about our lives is

> Peace and choice come from realizing that I give
> everything all the meaning it has for me.

To understand today's lesson, visually scan the room in which you now are. Start with things that are close to you and apply the lesson, in boldface, to all things upon which your eyes rest (large or small, people or objects, bright or dull). Then widen your gaze and look all around you, near and far, and apply the idea to everything you see, hear, taste, smell, or feel. Do not try to systematically include everything. Rather, just relax and apply the idea to anything that comes into your awareness. Do not decide to exclude anything either. Simply apply the idea in an equal fashion to everything, regardless of your seeming attachment or nonattachment to anyone or anything.

Say to yourself thoughts such as the following:

> I give this chair all the meaning that it has for me.
> I give these clothes all the meaning that they have for me.
> I give this person all the meaning they have for me.
> I give this substance (drug, food, alcohol, and so on)
> all the meaning that it has for me.

Periodically throughout the day practice applying the lesson. If you catch yourself operating in the addictive thought system, say:

> Peace comes from within me, and is not determined
> by people, places, or things.

LESSON TWO

My mind is preoccupied with past thoughts.

When you allow yourself to become burdened by guilt and shame, you are operating in the addictive thought system belief that the past always determines how you feel in the present. The love-based thought system recognizes that

It is impossible to feel guilt and love at the same time.

When feelings of guilt, shame, low self-esteem, or negative self-judgment arise, you can say to yourself,

I am not at peace because I am looking upon everything
and everyone through a distorting filter of the past.
Peace abides in the freedom of the present moment.

Whenever you identify with the past you preoccupy your mind and create blocks to experiencing love. When you use the past as a source of knowledge so that you can pass judgment and induce guilt, you further isolate yourself from love.

Today, be determined to break the cycle of addictive thinking. Begin by sitting comfortably with your eyes closed. Observe your mind. Note each thought as it comes and goes. Try not to spend too much time on any one thought. Simply watch your thoughts for a few minutes, with as little attachment as possible to each thought. Identify each thought by naming the central figure or theme of it. For example, as your thoughts come and go, say to yourself,

I am now thinking about (central figure or theme). And
now I am thinking about (central figure or theme).

As you observe your thinking, note how many of your thoughts are based in the past and potentially can produce guilt. After a few minutes of this, say to yourself,

> My mind is preoccupied with past thoughts. But the past is gone, and today I am willing to let it go. In the present moment I look upon myself with loving eyes.

If you find yourself in conflict during the day, say:

1. I'm in conflict because my mind is preoccupied with past thoughts.
2. But the past is gone.
3. Therefore, I choose to see this (situation/person/object) only in the peace of the present moment.

LESSON THREE

I am not the victim of the world I see.

The addictive thought system tells you that other people or circumstances are responsible for how you feel. You may be a habitual finger pointer, always playing the role of the victim. When you think that you are a victim of the world, you give up your personal power and the ability to choose.

In order to recognize your personal power, and to understand that you have choice, today focus upon a simple fact:

I am not a victim.
My own thoughts and beliefs
determine what I see and what I experience.

Begin your practice with the following:

When I see the world as responsible for how I feel, I am seeing myself as a victim, and consistent peace is impossible. Regardless of the circumstances I find myself in, I can maintain my power to choose.

When I am stuck in a rut, it may be because I am seeing myself as a victim. Today, if I feel victimized, I will not attack another or defend myself. Instead, I will remind myself,

I am not a victim of the world I see. I choose the feelings
I experience, and I decide upon my own goals.

The Addictive Thought System says, Changing others is how I am released from being a victim.

You choose the peaceful alternative when you recognize the truth:

Changing my mind—seeing that I am not a victim—is how
I am released from being a victim.

LESSON FOUR

I could see peace instead of this.

You are constantly choosing between the addictive thought system and the love-based thought system. You are always only a choice away from peace. Today's lesson focuses on the fact that you have the ability to direct your mind.

Peace of mind begins in your own mind. When you are not peaceful, it is because your eyes are closed to love. In addiction you see yourself as separate from others in a world that appears to be harsh, without meaning, threatening, and fragmented. You end up seeing yourself as vulnerable and in constant need of defense. But you can choose instead to see a united world where every situation offers you the opportunity to learn of love.

If you become depressed, sad, angry, guilty, or fearful, say to yourself,

I can choose peace *right now* instead of this.

If you find yourself caught in the addictive cycle of judging yourself or others, stop and silently say, I want peace of mind. Instead of judging, I choose to practice forgiveness.

By concentrating on forgiveness you train your mind to know where to look for peace. You come to understand that there is no need to wait any longer for peace of mind, because forgiveness is a choice you can make each minute of the day.

To demonstrate and ensure my choice for peace,
let all my actions be gentle and loving.

LESSON FIVE

Let me recognize the problem so it can be solved.

The addictive thought system says that in order to solve your problems and be happy you need to change someone or some circumstance. It also tells you that acquiring something new will lessen your problems. The last thing the addictive thought system would have you do is look at the contents of your thoughts, for this would reveal the flimsy foundation of the addictive thought system. The addictive thought system presents you with endless problems to be solved, yet always keeps the real problem hidden.

You cannot solve a problem if you do not know what it is. Today, instead of seeing yourself as having a number of problems to solve, concentrate on recognizing the one problem that is at the root of all others: the belief that you are unworthy of love, separate from love, alone, and empty.

This belief is the only problem that needs to be addressed, because it is from feeling of emptiness and unworthiness that leads you to look outside of yourself for happiness.

The addictive thought system has many costumes, which gives the illusion of many problems in need of many solutions. Today, be determined to look beyond the cloaks and masks and see the real problem. Seeing the underlying consistency to all problems is the first step to realizing that you have the means to solve them.

Sit comfortably and close your eyes. Tell yourself, my only problem is that I feel empty and so look outside of myself for happiness. As you allow your mind to become more quiet, the awareness of love will replace the endless list of worries. One by one, gently release the numerous problems you think you have from your mind. As you let go of each "problem," begin to feel the tranquility that comes from ceasing worry. Tell yourself, Whatever the problem, love is the answer.

When problems arise, you can say to yourself,

> Let me not be deceived about what the problem is here.
> Let me recognize that the real problem is my lack of an
> awareness of love.
> I invite love to make itself known to me.

You can also say to yourself,

> Today I see boundless love
> where yesterday I saw endless problems.

LESSON SIX

Forgiveness offers everything I want.

The addictive thought system tells you that constant analysis and judgment ensures your safety. But these activities are born of fear and only perpetuate fear. Today, instead of judging, choose to practice the gentle means that uproots the addictive thought system: forgiveness.

Sometimes you may be confused about what you want, and unsure of your life purpose. Peace does not come from the transient satisfaction of getting what you want. Consistent peace of mind is possible only through forgiveness. When you judge another as guilty you reinforce your own sense of guilt and unworthiness. This is because what you see are your own thoughts projected outward.

Forgiveness is always the peaceful solution. Forgiveness, being based on unity, recognizes that to free another from the chains of the past is to unbind yourself as well. In short, forgiveness is the water that extinguishes the raging fire of the addictive thought system.

Today, begin to use forgiveness as a means to bring about peace. Start by thinking of someone you dislike or see as having done something "unforgivable" to you. Close your eyes and picture this person standing in front of you. Tell yourself that only the present moment matters. Look upon this person as if you know nothing of his or her "wrongdoing." Notice a pray of light in this once fearful and hateful picture. Allow this light to spread, permeating and surrounding this person, until you hold a mental image bright and unmarred by the past. Hold this image in your mind for a few minutes. Notice, as you release the past and allow light to fill and surround this person, how peaceful you feel. After a few minutes, open your eyes and tell yourself,

Forgiveness offers everything I want.

Anytime you are upset during the day you can tell yourself,

As peace is my single goal, forgiveness is my function.

LESSON SEVEN

All that I give is given to myself.

The addictive thought system makes no connection between what you think and how you feel about yourself. You may not realize that your thinking determines your experience, but your thoughts are like a boomerang, always coming back to you.

Today, embrace the idea that giver and receiver are the same, that what you put out you receive back. Imagine what life would be like today if you had no goal besides peace, saw no value in negative judgment. You would be giving yourself the gift of peace of mind.

In your communication with others, if you offer acceptance, understanding, honesty, and forgiveness, you will find peace. If you offer judgment, attack, fear, and condemnation, you will be inviting distance and pain into your life. Examine your own past communications to see how this simple truth operates. Then start fresh today by saying to yourself,

Today I want peace and so I will offer only this to others.
Today I choose to hold love in my heart for others. I do so not
because I am superior or because I am inferior, but
because offering love is how I receive love.

Now close your eyes and spend a few minutes thinking of people in your life while focusing on deepening your love for them. Another helpful thing to do is to ask yourself,

Am I, *right now*, giving what I want for myself?

If not, simply change your mind and begin giving to others what you want for yourself.

LESSON EIGHT

I will not value what is valueless.

Nothing, in and of itself, has value. You determine what you feel is valuable and what is not. When you assign so much value to something that it results in an external pursuit of happiness, you are operating in the addictive thought system. This is important to remember, for you may behave as though you can't live without something, forgetting that you gave it all of the value that it has for you.

Once you realize that valuing the valuable ensures peace and valuing the valueless creates conflict, you are on the path to peace of mind. Yet what are the criteria for deeming something either valuable or valueless? Today's lesson addresses this question.

What you value determines what you want. Following is a list of criteria by which to judge all things that you think you want. No matter how much you want something, if it does not meet all these requirements, it has the potential to bring you conflict.

1. Will what I want last forever?

If not, it is valueless. Love, for example, is eternal, and is therefore valuable. Time can never diminish its value. Yet it is important to realize that it is not the impermanent things in themselves that bring pain, it is your attachment to them that creates addiction and conflict. Ask yourself, If I lost (specify), would my peace of mind be affected?

2. Will getting what I want result in someone else's loss?

If it will, it is valueless and will not bring you lasting happiness. If you seek to take something away from somebody, or harm another in any way, you have deceived yourself into thinking that another's loss and pain can be your gain. To give is to receive. To take at another's expense only harms myself.

3. Why is what I want of value to me?

Arms can be used to strike in anger or embrace in love. An airplane can drop bombs or packages of food. If you want peace, use all things as a means to create peace. Things are, in and of themselves, not bad, but attachment to them makes you a slave to them.

That which you value is that which you think will bring happiness, yet pursuit of it may result in frustration, depression, loss, and despair. When this happens it is probably because you have placed value on the valueless. Perhaps you think that things like money or prestige will give your life meaning. But when you look to them for happiness you are valuing the valueless and will always end up in conflict. If you want peace today, do not value the valueless.

LESSON NINE

If I defend myself I am attacked.

When you operate from the addictive thought system, you busy yourself building walls of defense and are always on the lookout for attack. Love becomes lost. How can your heart be open to love when it lies behind a fortress of fear?

When you defend yourself, you believe that your defense, if strong enough, will protect you. Perhaps, when hurt, you are quick to erect defenses. But those defenses keep you isolated and afraid. Your walls of defense lock out what you want the most: love.

You are mistaken if you think that your defenses protect you. In fact, your defenses simply help perpetuate the cycle of attack and defense. Nobody builds defenses who does not have fear in his or her heart.

You make defenses because you fear attack. Yet with each new defense, your fear of attack increases. How can defenses offer safety when they escalate fear? Today, recognize the truth about defenses:

Defenses always bring what they were meant to guard against.

Defensiveness sets up a cycle in which you cannot be peaceful. Attack leads to defense and defense leads to attack:

ATTACK

DEFENSE

Today, instead of making your armor thicker, invite love to replace your defenses. Love needs no defense. Love grows through being shared and is unaffected by time. Waiting for you, beneath your defenses, is undisturbed peace. It is this peace you can find today.

A good thing to remind yourself of throughout the day is

If I defend myself I am attacked.
Love is what I want and love needs no defense.
Today I offer love instead of defensiveness.

LESSON TEN

The power of decision is my own.

Your ability to choose is what constitutes your freedom. The power to decide which thoughts you hold in your mind is the richest gift you have, for it makes you the director of your life. You are always choosing between the addictive thought system and the love-based thought system. The decision you make determines your experience. Today, make this process of choosing conscious, and come to realize the power of decision.

You decide what to believe and thus choose your experience. It is not the world that molds and shapes you; you do it yourself. If you are in conflict, it is because you have accepted a false belief as true.

You are the director of your life. You decide between a script containing only scenes of peace and a horror story with terror and attack lurking in every corner. Your power of decision is a tool that you may have forgotten how to use to your benefit. Today, learn that your power of decision can ensure your peace of mind.

> The power of decision is my own.
> Today, I use this power to
> choose only love-based thoughts.

There is a quiet place within you that is undisturbed, full of love, and complete. When you quiet your mind you can hear this inner love guiding your way. Many refer to this inner guidance as their Higher Power, in contrast with the lower voice of the ego. Today, if you find yourself in conflict, you can say,

> Right now my power of decision can change how I feel.
> I can choose to listen to my Higher Power
> instead of the confusing chatter of the ego.

LESSON ELEVEN

Today I learn to give as I receive.

The addictive thought system wants you to believe that the more you get, take, buy, and conquer, the better you will feel. The emphasis is always on getting, never on giving. In the addictive thought system, giving is a manipulation, a way to get something that you want. The addictive thought system says that to give something is to lose something. In contrast, the love-based thought system says that to give is to receive.

In others you but see yourself. If you see others as having done unforgivable things, so must you see yourself. If you look upon one person or one thousand with condemnation and hate, so must you condemn and hate yourself. Likewise, when you see others through the soft, loving eyes of forgiveness, so must you love and forgive yourself.

There is not lapse of time between giving and receiving. As you give, so do you receive. This is why peace is always a possible alternative. Today's lesson offers the alternative to loneliness because

You can give and receive forgiveness and love at
any moment you so choose.

Today's lesson is very practical. You can easily and continually try it and verify the benefits throughout your day. As you see the effectiveness and results of giving and receiving love, the truth of giving and receiving will unfold to you.

Today, offer love, kindness, and compassion to everyone you meet or think about, and see how quickly the awareness of love returns to you. Begin the day by closing your eyes and saying to yourself,

To give is to receive.
I will receive what I am giving now.

Then picture in your mind a specific person and say, for example,

> To this person I offer peace of mind.
> To this person I offer tranquility.
> To this person I offer calmness.

Again, try not to exclude anyone today from the gifts you give. In the end, any exclusion is an exclusion of yourself. Every person you meet today offers you another chance for peace. If you find yourself hostile or defensive, ask yourself,

> Is this what I want to give myself?

LESSON TWELVE

I rule my mind, which I alone must rule.

The addictive mind is like a wild animal thrashing about uncontrollably. Today, begin to tame your unruly mind by realizing that you determine the thoughts that you think and thus the feelings that you have.

At times it may seem that you have no control over your life. Thoughts fly through your mind and you never question your beliefs. Instead of looking inward you begin to think that other people are the cause of your anger, fear, unhappiness, and depression. When you believe this, you cease to be the ruler of your own mind. Take the first step in deciding to rule your mind by taking responsibility for your own feelings and thoughts.

Today, understand that you alone rule your mind, choosing between the voice of the ego and the voice of love, deciding what thoughts to have, how to feel, and how to act. Today, determine to listen to the ever present peaceful preference within.

If you are to have peace, you first must take charge of your own mind. You can always direct your mind to recognize, listen to, and choose the peaceful alternative.

Whenever you experience an unwanted thought, you can silently say,

I rule my mind, which I alone must rule.
I choose to let go of this addictive belief (specify)
and direct my mind toward love.

LESSON THIRTEEN

Today I will judge nothing that occurs.

Judging others and yourself increases fear and guilt, shutting the door on love. Begin today by asking yourself the following questions:

1. If I stopped judging for one day, what would that day be like?
2. If I chose to concentrate on extending compassion instead of judgment, how would my experience change?
3. If I devoted a day to love rather than judgment, how would I feel around other people?

The thoughts that you hold toward others affect how you feel about yourself. For example, you cannot simultaneously feel hatred toward someone and feel love for yourself. It would be like trying to exhale and inhale in the same moment. You may have previously learned that it is both natural and healthy to judge situations and people, that it enables you to make good decisions. Today, begin to retrain your mind to see that your negative judgments do nothing but create feelings of separateness. Love-based thinking recognizes that any thought or action that condemns results in fear, guilt and aloneness.

Today, leave love free to exist undisturbed by your judgments. Instead of judging and separating, look at the interdependency of all life, of which you are an integral part.

Determine to view all people and events without negative judgment. When tempted to pass judgment, you can remind yourself,

If I judge this person
I will rob myself of love.

Begin to turn inward and allow love to be your guide.

Today, turn away from your old habit of
judgment and condemnation.
In looking for guidance, turn your focus inward,
toward your heart.
Trade the sword of judgment
for the tender touch of love,
and peace will dawn in your mind.

LESSON FOURTEEN

Let me not see myself as limited.

The addictive thought system promotes limitation in every way possible. The ego constantly tells you that you are full of lacks that can be filled only by someone or something outside yourself: a person, a drug, or a possession. Today, devote yourself to seeing yourself as whole, boundless, and with unlimited potential. Only your beliefs limit you. The only limits you have are self-imposed.

All thoughts of limitation are restrictive to relationships. When you place limits upon others, you bind yourself as well. There is no greater gift you can give than letting go of limitations. By doing so you unshackle yourself and others.

You may have limited yourself by perceiving darkness and weakness within and around yourself. Every limit that you impose on yourself or others is a chain that inhibits your growth. Today, give yourself strength by seeing the power of love everywhere and in everything.

Limits, which are created by the addictive thought system, appear very real. But regardless of the limitation the solution is the same: remember that you lack nothing to experience love this instant.

Today, begin to challenge any limitation, no matter how real it appears. For example, inadequate time and money are common lacks the addictive thought system invents. You may think that you do not have enough time to pause to relax, or perhaps not enough money to be happy and secure. Whenever you impose a limitation on yourself you can challenge it. For example, if you feel you lack time or money, you might say to yourself,

I am limitless.
Do I not have the time to send a loving thought?
Can I not afford to extend compassion from my heart?

The specific words are not important as long as you question the validity of every limit you have imposed, or are tempted to set. Especially question any phrase which can complete the following sentence: "Love is not possible now because ___."

The most important thing that you have to do today is to remember to remind yourself hourly:

I am not limited.
Love is with me now.

LESSON FIFTEEN

This day I choose to spend in perfect peace.

The addictive thought system says that the only way to spend a day in peace would be to have all of your emotional needs met by someone, have many material possessions, and be able to control all situations. The problem is that the list of needs becomes endless, the desire to control becomes compulsive, and peace becomes impossible. Today, understand that that is not the way to peace.

Peace has never left your mind. Have faith that peace is within you now; it is only covered by a thin veil of addictive thoughts. Today, look past this veil and rest in the quiet peace that awaits you. Today's lesson is a declaration that inner peace is possible if you just give it a chance to emerge. Instead of listening to your addictive thoughts today, make peace of mind your single goal.

It may not seem possible to you to spend an entire day in peace. Perhaps you think that if you were in a more ideal circumstance, then you could have peace. Such an "if-only . . ." thought system leads nowhere but to conflict. Reverse this thought system by telling yourself many times throughout the day:

Right now I have everything I need to have peace of mind.
If peace of mind is my single goal today,
what would I do now to ensure it?

The following are just a few examples of ways to ensure a day grows in peace:

1. Reach out to heal a relationship that has been wounded.
2. Let go of an ancient grudge.
3. Focus on giving instead of getting.
4. Extend a thought of compassion when you normally might defend yourself or judge someone.
5. Do something nurturing for yourself.

Make your own list and commit yourself to carrying it out.

LESSON SIXTEEN

I will not be afraid of love today.

The addictive thought system leads you down a path that results in your fearing love. In a mind full of guilt, fear, and judgment, the light of love is obscured by layers of darkness. Guilt keeps you from love, because you think that you are undeserving of it. Today, choose to welcome that which can heal you of all your misconceptions about yourself: love.

The foundation of your belief system is simple: you, like all people, identify with what you think will make you safe. If you use the addictive thought system you think that judgment, defenses, and attack are the keys to safety, and so you identify yourself with fear. If you use the love-based thought system you see that your safety lies in acceptance, forgiveness, and defenselessness, and so you identify yourself with love. What you choose to identify with— fear or love—will determine your feelings about yourself and your outlook on the world.

Today, invite truth into your mind. You have, no doubt, grown tired of the illusions of the addictive thought system. Love is your safety. Fear cannot exist where love is present.

When you identify with love you feel safe. When fear is your guide you constantly run to or from someone or something. Today, hold the invitation to love in your heart. Remind yourself hourly:

> Identify with love and I am safe.
> Identify with love and I am home.
> Identify with love and I find my Self.

Today, see the truth about fear by recognizing its presence in your life. When fear arises, face it. As you do, you will find that fear does not exist separate from the mind that made it. You give fear all the power it has. Fear does not exist in and of itself; it is formed and fueled by your thoughts. When you find yourself fearful, you can say to yourself,

> Only my mind can produce fear.
> Fear is overcome when I
> allow love to be itself.
> I welcome love today.

LESSON SEVENTEEN

I can be hurt by nothing but my thoughts.

Realizing the truth of this simple statement is the first step toward freedom. It is the prescription for healing your addictive mind. In the past, when you have been hurt, you may have looked to others as the cause of your pain. Or perhaps you blamed your unhappiness on bad luck or bad situations. Today, reverse this way of thinking by realizing that you can be hurt by nothing but your own thoughts.

When you find yourself in pain of any kind, it is helpful to examine your thoughts. This will help begin to heal the only thing that can hurt you in any way: your mind.

> Because my thoughts create the world I see and
> experience, it is with my thoughts that I must work.

I can change my thoughts about the world, about others, and about myself.

> I cannot change other people or many of the
> situations in which I find myself.

When you are hurt it is because you have accepted an addictive thought as true. You are always, every second of every day, choosing the thoughts that fill your mind and thus are choosing how you will feel. When you focus your attention on your thoughts, you can learn to choose the contents of your mind, and, in turn, what you feel. If you do not become aware of your thoughts you will continue to feel that you have no choice as to what you experience.

Stop letting the addictive thought system rule your mind. Today, consciously choose what thoughts to hold in your mind. In this way you can direct your mind away from hurt and toward love.

You can begin to direct your mind by practicing the following process:

1. Whenever you find yourself anything other than peaceful, identify the addictive thought that you are holding in your mind.
2. Tell yourself that this thought is causing you pain and keeping love buried in darkness.
3. Turn inward and tell yourself,

Who I am is love.
I can elect to change this addictive thought.

LESSON EIGHTEEN

Let me remember what my purpose is.

If you were always aware of your true purpose—love and forgiveness—there would be no reason to listen to the irrationality of the addictive thought system. It is in remembering your purpose that love can begin to shine in your mind. Today, concentrate on remembering love, instead of being bound by the chains of fear.

When you forget that your goal is peace of mind, you become confused and conflicted, unsure of your direction, and, ultimately, unsure of who you are. When you forget your purpose, you become like a robot, automatically responding to external circumstances while having many conflicting goals. When you forget that your purpose is forgiveness, you judge others. In the absence of the awareness of love you become concerned with getting instead of giving, condemning instead of accepting. You become obsessively involved in pursuing that which is valueless. You have conflicted goals if you tell yourself that you want love, yet, at the same time, have a goal to change others to fit your specifications. Conflicting goals never lead to love.

When I have conflicting goals,
conflict is what I'll get.

The addictive thought system specializes in conflicting goals. These conflicting goals can make you depressed, frustrated, fearful, and angry. You can escape from conflicting goals by identifying which goal is bringing you pain. Release that goal and keep the one you know brings love. The key to remembering your purpose is to discipline your mind to identify and let go of what does not lead to love. An unexamined mind goes unchanged.

You can escape the pain of conflicting goals by determining to remember your purpose. You can tell yourself,

What I want is love.
To have love I offer love—
and forgiveness is how I offer it.

LESSON NINETEEN

My present happiness is all I see.

When you look at yourself through the window of the past, it is like looking in a curved amusement park mirror: you see a distorted image of yourself. With each new breath you move into a new moment, untouched by the past. Today your goal is to embrace your happiness through living in this new moment. The only thing that you need to do to see your happiness is to change your mind from being focused on the past to being focused on the present. The present moment is a beautifully wrapped gift of love. It is waiting for you to open it.

Only when you look upon a distorted past and anticipate a fearsome future does your present happiness escape you. When you see a world full of separation, what you see is painful and frightening. Do not allow yourself to be deceived into thinking that guilt is inescapable, because in the present moment guilt does not exist. Today, begin to see that there is no value in holding onto the past.

Throughout this day, seek to find nothing but your present happiness, and look upon only what you seek. Do not obsessively wish that something could be different, and don't invite fear into your mind by thinking that the future will duplicate the past. Realize that the only thing that keeps you from experiencing peace of mind is your procrastination in accepting it, for peace of mind is always available to you in the present moment.

Repeat to yourself often:

The past is past.
The future is in the future.
My present happiness is all I see.

LESSON TWENTY

This instant is the only time there is.

Today's lesson is an extension of yesterday's in that the emphasis is upon living in the present moment. When your mind is focused on love, the present moment is all that exists in your awareness. Fear is a stranger to the love-based thought system. In contrast, the addictive thought system uses the past as a branding iron, attempting to burn guilt deep into your mind.

If you want a tranquil mind you must change your idea about the purpose of time. You may have seen time as both a judge and a prison guard, sentencing you to the guilt of the past and the worry of the future, overlooking the serenity of the present moment. Such a conception of time defeats your goal of inner peace and hides love from your awareness. How you perceive time determines what you will experience.

Emphasis upon the past produces guilt.
Emphasis upon the future produces worry and fear.
Emphasis upon the present yields love.

You may mistakenly have thought that love was something to be achieved. You may have put love off into the future by thinking that you had to do something to be loved. Love is not achieved, love is remembered in the present moment. It is in the eternal now that love waits patiently. You may have thought that you had to wait for certain things to be accomplished or changed in order to deserve love; the only thing that needs to change is your belief about time.

When I am anything less than joyous,
when I feel a lack of any kind,
when I want something I don't have,
when I think that peace is impossible
because of what has happened,
or that peace is impossible
because of what has not happened,
I need but remind myself:

I need to change my mind about time.
This instant is the only time there is.

LESSON TWENTY-ONE

Fear binds the world, forgiveness sets it free.

Today's idea is a summarization: within this lesson are all the other ideas presented in this book.

The addictive thought system of fear, judgment, and guilt bind you in conflict and pain. The love-based thought system of caring, forgiveness and peace heals your mind and cleanses your perception.

Choose to break the bars of the prison of fear and realize how much all people are alike. Today, allow the darkness of conflict to be healed by the light of forgiveness. No longer can separation, fear, and conflict be called by other names, denied, projected onto someone or something else, avoided, hidden, or disguised.

Blocks to forgiveness, and, therefore, love, arise when you accept the addictive thought system as true. As you gently remove these obstacles, the awareness of love becomes free to blossom and grow.

Determine to no longer hold yourself and the world in fear. Today, use no relationship, object, or situation to hold yourself in the past. Instead, in all situations, and with all whom you meet, see that another chance for peace given to you. With each new moment you can ensure your peace of mind by practicing forgiveness.

With all whom you see or think about, offer a gentle thought of forgiveness, and accept the same for yourself.

Fear binds the world.
Forgiveness sets it free.
This is the key to my healing.

Epilogue

It is a wonderful morning, and I am sitting upon a sun-swept hillside near my home in Carmel Valley. The poetry of the wind through the trees is accented by the distant sound of wind chimes sending messages of tranquility. My dog, Vali, lies by my side, panting. Carny is three months pregnant, and my heart awaits welcoming a new being into our lives and the world. Today feels happy and gentle. It is in this spirit that I would like to leave you, the reader.

Much of my life I felt that my heart was dying a slow death, that I had no choice but to slip deeper into the hopeless despair of fear. Though at times I still experience fear and all of its terror, I am now able to more consistently choose love. This day I feel alive. I feel open and unguarded. Today I choose love and union over fear and separateness. Today I know that there is not a being on this planet who is not deserving and in need of love, kindness, and compassion. May I learn to live my life knowing that this is the only truth.

Peace to you and may your path be blessed.

UNFOLDING

Love always surrounds us in gentility,
yet we so often turn our backs,
walking aimlessly into darkness.

May we cease this futile pattern
and surrender to the serenity of love,
breathe in the joy of life.
Let us pass our days smiling upon each other
while extending our hands in kindness and forgiveness.
May we speak from the center of our being,
and allow others to know our hearts.
May we each feel the limitless depth
of love that abides in and around us,
and know that this is who we are.

About the Author

Dr. Lee Jampolsky is a licensed psychologist in private practice in Monterey, California. He is a consultant to various treatment programs for chemical dependency. He founded the outpatient program at the Community Hospital Recovery Center and Clint Eastwood Adolescent Program, now listed as one of the one hundred best programs nationally. He has taught at several universities in the areas of addiction and conflict resolution. Dr. Jampolsky also founded the first state-approved doctoral program in peace studies. He has been on numerous radio and television programs, speaking on chemical dependency, relationships, and the psychology of peace and conflict resolution. Additionally, he has spoken to a variety of professional groups, including the American Psychological Association. He lives in Carmel Valley, California, with his wife, Carny, and their daughter Jalena.

More books that can help

☐ *Recovery from Addiction* by John Finnegan and Daphne Grey

Alternative herbal and nutritional therapies for a wide range of addictions, from cigarettes to sugar to caffeine to hard drugs. Includes first-person accounts of how these treatments have worked for a variety of specific problems.

$9.95 paper, 192 pages

☐ *Choose to be Healthy* by Susan Smith Jones, Ph.D.

The choices we make in life can greatly increase our health and happiness—this book details how to analyze one's choices about food, exercise, thought, work, and play, and then use this information to create a better, healthier life.

$9.95 paper, 252 pages

☐ *Love Is Letting Go of Fear* by Gerald Jampolsky, M.D.

One of the most popular New Age books ever. The lessons in this little book based on *A Course in Miracles*, will teach you to let go of fear and remember that our true essence is love. Includes daily exercises for personal transformation. Over 1,000,000 copies in print.

$7.95 paper or $9.95 cloth, 144 pages

☐ *Unlimit Your Life* by James Fadiman, Ph.D.

How to assess and understand the factors holding you back in life, and then set concrete goals—personal, economic, career, or spiritual—and start attaining them in the most effective, satisfying way possible.

$9.95 paper, 224 pages

Available from your local bookstore, or order direct from the publisher. Please include $1.25 shipping & handling for the first book, and 50 cents for each additional book. California residents include local sales tax. Write for our free complete catalog of over 400 books and tapes.

Ship to:

Name_____

Address_____

City_____ State ____ Zip _____

Phone _____

Celestial Arts

Box 7327

Berkeley, CA 94707

For VISA or Mastercard orders

call (510) 845-8414